Lincoln Christian College
P9-BZW-533

Church Family Camps and Conferences

Church Family Camps and Conferences

An Administrative and Program Manual

ELIZABETH AND WILLIAM H. GENNÉ

THE CHRISTIAN EDUCATION PRESS
Philadelphia

Prepared at the request of the
Committee on Camps and Conferences
and the Committee on Family Life
of the Division of Christian Education
National Council of the Churches of Christ

THE CHRISTIAN EDUCATION PRESS
Library of Congress Catalog Card Number 62-9970

To Four Good Campers

NAN, TOM, PEG, and SUE

CONTENTS

INTRODUCTION

DURING RECENT years we have seen a rapid growth in family camps and family conferences under church auspices. As in every rapidly growing movement, there has been considerable experimentation with a wide variety of ideas. The variety has been so wide that some ideas have been contradictory and this has created a situation of considerable confusion. Another contributing factor has been the tendency to use the words "family camp" and "family conference" interchangeably.

This book has been written to help churches to realize the value in both the camp experience and the conference experience as part of their total ministry to families. Families, as well as individuals, need Christian education and we might well consider the contribution camps and conferences can make to the achievement of our educational purpose, which may be stated as follows:

> The objective for Christian education is that all persons [and families] be aware of God's self-disclosure, especially his redeeming love as revealed in Jesus Christ, and that they respond in faith and love—to the end that they may know who they are and what their human situation means, grow as sons [children] of God, rooted in the Christian community, live in the Spirit of God in every relationship, fulfill their common discipleship in the world, and abide in the Christian hope.*

This book also has the purpose of helping churches to think more clearly and distinctly about these two types of experience and to choose for each occasion the one better suited to achieve the goals and objectives

* From "An Objective of Christian Education for Senior High Young People," a study document of the Division of Christian Education of the National Council of Churches.

sought. Of course, both the camp and the conference as presently conceived allow for considerable flexibility. It is possible to incorporate certain features of each into the other. It is helpful, however, to know which is which, lest we develop a hopelessly confused muddle.

The family camping movement owes a great debt to the developments in camping among children and youth. Among the emphases which camping stresses are:

1. The educational value of the real-life situations which emerge when a person or group seeks to live in the out-of-doors
2. The educational value of a more flexible schedule to take full advantage of these emerging situations
3. The educational value of the small group in an intimate living experience

Family conferences have come out of a different background. Churches in America have long known the "camp meeting," the chautauqua lectures, the Bible and missions institutes, and similar gatherings which sought to bring together as many people as possible for enlightenment and inspiration and which placed considerable emphasis on teaching and preaching.

In order to handle such large groups, rather elaborate schedules, programs, and forms of organization were developed. Large conference centers were built with cottages, assembly and dining halls, and planned recreational areas. In recent years, however, in line with sound educational principles, family conferences have tended to limit their size and have included more small discussion groups.

The chapters which follow have been prepared especially for the family life committees of local congregations and of the state and area committees of denominations and councils of churches in order to help them in the development of their programs for family camps and conferences. They have also been prepared for those selected to give staff leadership to such programs.

As indicated in the text, the sponsoring committee should decide the basic policies and goals of any project and select the leadership for it. Then the leadership staff should develop the program in harmony with those policies and goals. We hope the suggestions that follow will prove a valuable resource to both the sponsoring committees and the staffs.

One word of caution needs to be added regarding our fundamental philosophy of working with families. There has been something of a fad or bandwagon psychology about family programs developing as many educational and community agencies, including the church, have come to recognize the primary importance of the family.

Some of these organizations have sincerely developed programs which have been genuine and helpful to families. Others have seemed to exploit families for their own institutional aggrandizement.

Churches have not been completely free from this temptation to institutional self-centeredness. Some have promoted a lot of so-called "family" activity which was really designed to further the institutional needs of the church as an organization.

Other instances have been marked by confusion or unclear thinking. There has been a tendency to label Bible study conferences, missions institutes, leadership schools, and any number of other events as "Family . . ." this or that, when they have nothing to do with family matters.

If a congregation wants to have a supper to discuss its budget and finance campaign, that is all well and good, but it is putting on a "church" supper, not a "family" supper.

If a denomination or a council wants to train leaders for its organization, or to increase missions giving, it may hold a conference, but it will not be a family conference just because families happen to be invited.

The term "family" should be used to identify only those experiences which are designed to strengthen and enrich family life in its primary relationships.

Recently we were invited to share in the leadership of a so-called family conference. Further inquiry revealed that the primary purpose of the conference was to train leaders for various aspects of the educational program of the churches. Parents spent the greater portion of each day in classes and preparing assignments to earn credits toward a certificate. Younger children were the demonstration students in the laboratory school. Adolescent sons and daughters were housed and fed in a separate area and had a completely independent youth program of their own. To top it off, it was made clear to us that if we wanted to bring our own children they would have to accept these arrangements. It seemed clear to the two of us that we were being invited to talk *about* family life rather than to enter into an experience of family living with our own and other families.

To label such a conference a "family conference" seemed to us to border on the dishonest. Let us be honest with our families. They will recognize and respond to the legitimate organizational needs of the church if, on other occasions, the church will recognize their legitimate family needs and minister to them.

The six of us in the Genné family look back over the years to experiences of living with families in camps or in conferences in Washington, Oregon, Colorado, Wisconsin, Michigan, Ohio, and New York. We have seen the growth and transformation that have taken place when a family has found itself in a community of Christian love.

We have seen that wonderful look in the eyes of children who in time of need could turn to any adult who happened to be near with the assurance of a loving response.

We have seen families rise to the crises of illness and accident and, indeed, whole groups of families help each other during epidemics.

We have heard preachers moved to say, "This week has helped my families more than a whole year of my preaching. And it has helped me understand them better than I ever could at home."

Because of these experiences, and many others like them, we are firmly convinced and enthusiastically committed to the value of the family camp and the family conference as part of the church's total ministry to families. If this book helps to make it possible for families to reach a similar conviction, it will have helped to answer our heartfelt prayer.

ELIZABETH AND WILLIAM GENNÉ

SCHEDULE OF PREPARATIONS

This schedule assumes a major event of a week or longer in duration. It is meant to serve as a step-by-step guide and checklist for committees sponsoring family camps or conferences, for directors, and for staff families.

	CAMPS	CONFERENCES
TWELVE MONTHS IN ADVANCE		
Sponsoring Committee		
1. Decides purposes and type of program	______	______
2. Selects site and dates	______	______
3. Determines budget and costs	______	______
4. Selects director-family and staff	______	______
NINE MONTHS IN ADVANCE		
Sponsoring Committee*		
1. Releases publicity	______	______
2. Plans promotion campaign	______	______
3. Completes selection of staff	______	______
SIX MONTHS IN ADVANCE		
Sponsoring committee pushes promotion campaign	______	______
Director-Family		
1. Develops letters, portrait sheets, etc., and begins correspondence as soon as families register	______	______

* Once director-family is selected, continuous consultation is assumed.

	CAMPS	CONFERENCES
2. Has get-acquainted contacts with staff in person or by correspondence	______	______
3. Consults with site management, clarifying their respective responsibilities	______	______

THREE MONTHS IN ADVANCE

Sponsoring committee continues promotion of registrations	______	______
Director-Family		
1. Corresponds with and gathers information from registrants	______	______
2. Calls meeting of leadership staff for inspection of site and pre-planning	______	______
3. Confirms staff responsibilities in writing	______	______
4. Arranges for ordering necessary program supplies	______	______
Staff families begin planning on basis of preliminary information from registrants	______	______

ONE MONTH IN ADVANCE

Sponsoring committee continues promotion of registrations	______	______
Director-Family		
1. Keeps correspondence with registrants up to date	______	______
2. Assigns living sites, if possible	______	______
3. Begins to involve registrants in some special responsibilities (worship planning, recreational leadership, etc.), as interests and abilities are discovered	______	______
4. Makes preliminary assignments to any work crews required (such as table waiters)	______	______
Staff families continue planning, if possible involving registrants as interests become known	______	______

	CAMPS	CONFERENCES
ONE WEEK IN ADVANCE		
Sponsoring committee consults with director-family on final details	______	______
Director-Family		
1. Checks on details of all preceding planning	______	______
2. Notifies staff of any late registrants	______	______
3. Checks staff on arrival time	______	______
Staff families assemble and pack supplies	______	______
ONE DAY IN ADVANCE		
Director and staff families arrive on site	______	______
OPENING DAY		
Director and staff families carry forward opening day plans	______	______
DAY FOLLOWING EVENT		
Staff families prepare evaluations	______	______
ONE WEEK AFTER EVENT		
Director-family submits summary of evaluations and recommendations for future program to the sponsoring committee	______	______
Sponsoring Committee		
1. Cleans up all financial responsibilities for past event	______	______
2. Receives recommendations for future program and begins making plans for any future events	______	______

ONE: THE CHURCH AND ITS FAMILIES

THE CHURCH'S CONCERN FOR FAMILIES

The church and the family have been, are, and always will be inextricably intertwined. Jesus was born into a family. His church spread across the then known world from home to home. "The church in your house" is a familiar New Testament phrase. (See Romans 16:5; 1 Corinthians 16:19; Philemon 2.)

The church today as it faces its mission of proclaiming the good news of Christ for our lives, must seek to understand the family and to minister to it in such an effective way that the family becomes a channel for the power of God's love in the lives of all of its members.

That families can become channels for God's love is a basic conviction of the church's work with families. Often the confusions, the perplexities, the failures, the frustrations of family life tend to overwhelm us to the point of despair. Deeper reflection, however, often discloses the outlines of God's purposes for Christian family life.

The child growing up in a home is surrounded by others of different ages, different abilities, and different interests. In the midst of the inevitable confusions, the child sees his pattern for growth in those who are older, he learns consideration for others, forgiveness, and the true meaning of love—if such love characterizes the relationships within the family.

All of the modern sciences are unanimous in their affirmation of the home as influencing the life of each individual and as constituting the basic unit for the perpetuation of the species and the transmission of the culture of any society. This does not mean that the influence is always good. Those families that are weak or distorted in their relationships may fall far short of a wholesome positive influence—indeed, they may be decidedly negative. Nevertheless, the primacy, intimacy, and importance of such relationships is basic in influencing the development of every person.

This then is the reason for the church's concern for and ministry to families. Whether the church's principal task is described as "evangelistic" or "educational"; as a "witness" or a "mission," or however else we choose to define it, the fact remains that it must deal with persons who live in families. The quality of the relationships within those families can be either a tremendous asset and ally of the church in its task, or it can be a powerful obstacle. Certainly the church cannot afford to ignore or neglect this aspect of its ministry.

HOW DOES THE CHURCH HELP FAMILIES?

An effective ministry to families demands that the church and its leaders must seek to understand the purposes of God in the creation of man and woman. Their sexuality, with all of its complexities and all of its mysteries, must be accepted as a part of this purposive creation.

Each man and each woman must be helped to become aware of and to respond to God's love, and guided in the fulfillment of his manhood or her womanhood according to God's purpose or "vocation" for that person.

Husbands and wives must be helped to have a constantly growing relationship of love for each other, even when they tend to be preoccupied with child rearing. They should be guided toward an increasing fulfillment of their marriage, even on into the years of retirement.

Children need to be nourished physically and nurtured spiritually so that they have a healthy and wholesome regard for themselves, including their sexuality.

Youth need to be guided and inspired as they move out from self-awareness to the establishment of friendships with the complementary sex. (We prefer this word to "opposite" sex, which seems to imply some degree of opposition.)

Older youth need to be helped to understand the nature and goals of Christian marriage, and in the light of these goals, to select their marriage partners and lay the foundations for Christian home life.

Parents must be helped to understand the spiritual as well as the physical and intellectual dimensions of their parenthood so that they may fulfill their responsibilities for the Christian nurture of their children.

And families, those new unities created by marriage, always need to be guided and helped to recognize their responsibilities toward others in the community and world surrounding them. The family also has a purpose or "vocation" in God's plan. The family that is strong and healthy simply to enjoy itself is in danger of making an idol of "togetherness." The Christian family will seek to grow in health and strength in order that it may grow in service to God and his world-wide family.

When the church is willing to give itself in such a ministry it always finds the loyalty and commitment of a grateful people rising up to strengthen and enrich its life and mission as a church.

In this ministry the church uses many and varied methods, programs, materials, curricula, and experiences. In this book we look at two types of experiences in which increasing numbers of families have become interested, and which the church has found increasingly fruitful. These are the family camp and the family conference.

There is nothing in the wide world to prevent a family or a group of families from going off to some resort or on a camping trip entirely on their own without any plans such as are outlined on the following pages. We hope, if they are Christians, that their church would have given them some convictions and skills that would help them have the richest kind of experience on their own.

The purpose of this manual, however, is to help those churches, denominations, and councils which wish to offer a camp or conference type of experience as part of a total planned ministry to their families. This means that a group of families will go out under church or council sponsorship. To be of greatest value, both to the families and to the sponsor, this experience should be related in a responsible way to the congregation, to the area agency of the denomination, or to the council which sponsors it.

THE SPONSOR'S RESPONSIBILITIES

Many churches and councils now have a Family Life Committee. Sometimes this is a committee with full and regular standing in its own right which includes representatives of the various units of the organization. In a few instances it is a subcommittee of the social service or fellowship department. Most usually it is a subcommittee of the educational unit of the agency. Whatever its organizational status may be, the unit conducting the family camp or conference should have a clear-cut line of responsibility and should be broadly representative of the total life and work of the church or council.

It is the responsibility of this committee to determine the purposes and goals of the experiences it will offer to the families. Once the purposes have been clarified, it can select either the camping type of program or the conference type of program as the better method for achieving its ends. This decision will in turn help to determine the selection of a site, the selection of staff personnel, and the duration, size, and financial arrangements of the project. The committee also has the responsibility of promoting the project among its constituency.

During recent years considerable confusion has developed about the differences between camps and conferences. Many conference-type programs have been held on camp sites. Elements of camping programs have been developed within conference programs. Likewise, elements of conference programing have been used in some camps. Some sponsors have even used the hyphenated term camp-conference to describe their program. How can we distinguish between the two?

1. A conference may be held on a camp site, but it could, as far as its program schedule and activities are concerned, be held just as well at a resort hotel, a college campus, or in some similar setting. The out-of-doors is integral to the camping experience.

2. A conference may include some appreciation of God's out-of-doors and some skills in out-of-door living, but these are not essential to the daily living routines, as they are in a camp.

Both the family camp and the family conference are concerned with the strengthening and enrichment of Christian living within the family. Their methods and emphases vary.

In order to make this decision, the responsible committee of the sponsoring agency will want to consider carefully the descriptions of the camp-type and the conference-type experiences outlined in the following two chapters. They must also consider the needs and the readiness of the families in their constituency. They should keep clearly in mind the goals of Christian family life fostered by their church or agency. Then, in the light of these goals and needs, they should formulate the specific goals and objectives for their project and select the type of experience they consider better suited for their purpose.

SUGGESTIONS REGARDING PROMOTION

The announcement and promotion of either a family camp or a family conference will be quite similar. Therefore, before moving to a consideration of the details of organization and program of these two types of program, we would make the following suggestions regarding promotion which will be applicable to either.

The sponsoring committee, in consultation with the camp or conference director, is responsible for promoting the event.

Timing the announcement is very important. If summer vacation dates are involved, the announcements should be ready by the first day of December of the year preceding and certainly not later than the first day of January. The need for this is obvious, because father's vacation schedule must be cleared months in advance and the family will want to coordinate this event with other summer plans. Even weekend projects in local congregations need to be announced early enough so that all family members can clear their schedules.

Purposes should be clearly stated in all publicity. Since family programs are relatively new, explicit interpretation is required. It is not simply a cheap vacation, nor is it a military camp where everyone is routed at the crack of dawn by a sharp blast from the bugle. It is not a place to park the wife and kiddies while father goes fishing or golfing. It is an opportunity for whole families to grow together as they live with other families in a Christian community.

The most effective publicity is person-to-person. In a local congregation, the sponsoring committee should carefully arrange interviews with as many families, including the children, as possible in addition to the general announcements and printed or mimeographed materials.

Committees serving groups of churches in synods, conferences, state, or provincial organizations should try to arrange personal presentations, preferably by families who have already taken part in such a program. In inaugurating the first event, it is the responsibility of the committee to lend their personal support in this kind of face-to-face presentation. Once the program has gotten under way, families from one church will usually be willing to visit other nearby churches.

While general announcements have some value, presentations should be made to specific groups such as adult classes, women's societies, men's clubs, couple's clubs, and, of course, parent study classes.

Family events should have a separate and distinct leaflet which describes their values, objectives, and activities. General announcements of children's and youth programs cannot be expected to carry the interpretation of the family programs also, although family events may be listed there.

The leaflet in either printed or mimeographed form should be attractive and illustrated, if possible. It should be designed to answer all (or most!) of the questions of skeptical fathers, hesitant mothers, and curious children. It should include:

1. The purpose of the event, concisely stated
2. The place, with description of site (pictures or drawings, if possible), clear directions for travel, mail address, and phone number
3. Dates, with specific arrival and departure times
4. Sponsoring agency and address
5. Director's name and, if known, other staff
6. Costs, when enrollment fee is due, when balance is due, and listing of "extras," if any
7. General description of the program and the minimum ages of children welcomed
8. Information regarding health and safety certification and practices
9. What to bring: amount and type of bedding, clothing, other equipment
10. Enrollment blank with space to list parents' names, children's names, birth dates and grades in school, address, phone number, and, if necessary, home church and pastor's endorsement. Enrollment deadline date should be clearly indicated. If there is any possibility of misunderstanding, the policy on racial inclusiveness should be clearly stated also.

Such leaflets should be placed in the hands of parents or mailed to them individually with letters of invitation.

Visual aids are a potent means of promotion, especially when movies, slides, or pictures of actual family programs in progress can be shown. To promote the first event, visual aids can usually be borrowed from some nearby agency. Pictures of the living accommodations, dining hall, and waterfront are most influential in bringing about enrollments.

Early enrollments may be encouraged by having a cheaper registration fee for those who enroll before a certain date. A deadline of four weeks prior to the date of the event, should be set to encourage early decisions. Refunds can be made in case of illness or other family emergencies.

The enrollment blank should be returned to the director or forwarded to him at once upon receipt in the sponsor's office. As soon as the enrollment is received a process of communication should begin which can be vital in the success of the project.

The director will want to send immediately a word of greeting, some word about his own family (perhaps even a snap of them) and enclose a "family portrait sheet" (see Appendix C) for the family to return. This initial letter should be personalized. If mimeographed, it should provide for personalized salutation and signature and for some comments—for instance, that there are children of the same ages in the two families.

If there are young children in the enrolling family, an additional sheet may be enclosed giving information about food for youngsters, high chairs, whether or not cribs are available, provisions for laundering, and similar information. This might be signed by the director's wife and written in "mother-to-mother" fashion. (See Appendix D.)

After the portrait sheet has been returned, the director will note the interests and abilities of the various family members. The director may write asking them to bring some special craft or hobby equipment or to share in the leadership of the camp in some particular way. (Caution: while it is good to involve new people, some check should be made on their abilities before committing critical responsibilities to them.)

About a month or three weeks before the opening date the director should send a second letter (see Appendix B) to all enrolled, giving the names of the other staff families, confirming the time of the opening day (especially when the first meal will be served), and enclosing a suggested schedule for at least the first twenty-four hours. Also included in this letter should be information about where to report upon arrival and the procedure regarding health checks. If cabin or room assignments can be made in advance and a map of the site enclosed, interest will be heightened.

Some directors like to suggest that the family prepare a distinctive sign to be placed outside their cabin or tent. The children can often think of colorful, pictorial signs such as "The Byrd's Nest," "The Hutchinson's Hutch," or "Our Jackson's Hole." Usually such signs include figures and names for each family member so passersby will get acquainted with all the family members.

Some like to suggest that during the trip each family compose a jingle or song to be sung the first night. For this some have used:

Hi ho, hi ho,
It's off to camp we go,
____
____
Hi ho, hi ho.

Throughout all these preliminary communications, the joy of living and sharing together in this kind of experience is kept uppermost. It should be made clear that, while the schedule will be very relaxed and leisurely, it will nevertheless be an adventure in personal and family growth and that everyone will be expected to share in the leadership at some point.

Families who feel a personalized interest from the time they send in their registrations will be the best promotional agents for the following years.

THE FAMILY CAMP

TWO: PLANNING FOR A FAMILY CAMP

PURPOSES AND GOALS

The first national consultation of governmental and private agencies interested in family camping defined such camping as follows: "Family camping is an adventure in outdoor living. The family exercises its ingenuity in providing shelter, preparing food, and enjoying the natural environment."

Christian family camping is all this and much more! To paraphrase this definition, we might say: "Christian family camping is an adventure of living in God's out-of-doors. The family exercises its ingenuity in providing shelter, preparing food, and enjoying the natural environment to the end that all family members may have an increased awareness of God as Father and Creator, and of his love as revealed in Christ. Through their shared activity they become aware of the meaning of Christian cooperation and community, and are better able to express these values in their family living."

Some of the values of family camping have been described in the following contrasting statements:

1. Family camp helps us to realize our dependence on nature. We live close to the sources of food, water, and the other elements of our existence.

2. Family camp helps us to realize our independence. We get along with such few things that we wonder why we let our everyday life become so encumbered with material concerns.

3. Family camp helps us to realize our dependence on each other. Responsible cooperation and teamwork are essential.

4. Family camp helps us to realize our independence as we develop our own resourcefulness and confidence in out-of-doors living.

5. Family camp helps us realize the value of simple, communal life.

6. Family camp helps us to realize the inadequacy of a life concerned with only the physical necessities.

While keeping these basic definitions in mind, the sponsoring committee will need to remember that family camping may be conducted in a variety of ways. Families with children approaching adolescence or older and with experience in out-of-door skills may want to back-pack into the wilderness. Other families, less experienced and with younger children, will do better with a cabin as the base for their out-of-door explorations. In some tent-camping areas, families will cook all of their meals out-of-doors. At other camp sites there will be a central dining room for most meals, with cookouts arranged as they are desired.

The sponsoring committee will need to make its decisions in the light of its purposes and with due consideration of the needs and readiness of its families. If it decides on a camping experience, the committee will need to locate an adequate site.

STANDARDS

Site, Facilities, and Equipment

Local congregations may use accessible state, provincial, or national parks. YMCA, YWCA, or scout camp sites are often adaptable to family camping if their basic facilities can meet the standards. Camps that have cabins for six or eight campers can usually be adapted to family camping by assigning one family to each cabin. Barracks-like cabins or dormitory sleeping rooms are not suitable for families. Nor is it sufficient to hang a blanket or curtain between families. The basic requirement for a family camp site is that each family shall have privacy for its sleeping arrangements. They may share dining facilities and sanitary facilities, but each family needs and deserves a place of its own in which they can dress, sleep, and have opportunity for family discussions in private.

The sponsoring committee should use the check list in Appendix A to evaluate the physical facilities, living accommodations, food service, and sanitary facilities of any camp site under consideration. The check list is based on the standards of the American Camping Association and the Committee on Camps and Conferences of the National Council of the Churches of Christ in the U.S.A.

Duration, Size, and Cost

The length of time is an important element in the educational experience of any group. For families from the same congregation who already know each other, a well-planned weekend can be a very rich experience, but a whole week together would multiply the benefits. For families coming together from an area representing several local communities, five days should be regarded as a minimum. A full seven-day week would be preferable. Some camps are planned for ten days or two weeks.

A local church could sponsor a tent-camping weekend with three or more families at an established camp site. Where some operating overhead has to be figured in the cost, ten or a dozen families would constitute an ideal group. To exceed a maximum of twelve families, including the leader families, would create problems that impair the efficacy of the experience.

It is important that all members of the family household participate in the camp experience. This policy should be firmly adhered to. Fragments of families or part-time participation is not good for the family and disrupts the camp morale.

A minimum age for children should be agreed upon and clearly stated in all announcements and publicity. Our present knowledge and experience would indicate that camping activities are beyond the physical endurance and maturity level of children under five years of age. Families with children under five should be referred to a family conference or invited to wait until their children are at least five years old.

Financing a family camp will need the careful attention of the sponsoring committee. Because of each family's need for privacy, living accommodations usually cannot be filled as efficiently as when occupied by sex-segregated groups. Economic considerations should never be allowed to destroy privacy.

If the sponsoring agency is convinced of the value of this kind of experience, it will also make sure that any family, regardless of its size, is able to take advantage of it. Many camps in both the United States and Canada have established a "family rate" of about $65 to $75 per week regardless of the size of the family. This tends to insure the attendance by the total family unit.

Some camps have a sliding scale of fees graduated according to adults, teenagers, and children under twelve. Others use a consumer cooperative plan, charging a fixed fee for certain fixed costs, then sharing only the actual costs of food and other supplies.

Of course, in local church camps, the Christian education committee may provide the program expenses while each family brings its own tent and food.

If necessary, the sponsoring agency should try to arrange some subsidy for the family camp in order to keep the cost within the reach of all. In camps serving a large area, often the local church or agency will pay up to half the cost for each of its families. This has been found to be a good investment, because families usually come back with increased vitality and interest in the work of the church.

It should be unnecessary to add that careful records should be kept and sound financial procedures followed regarding purchases and the payments for expenses. Insurance for campers should be arranged. Agreements with site managements, staff, and any related personnel should be in writing.

Staff Personnel

Depending on the size and location of the camp, staff requirements will vary greatly. Three or four families from a local congregation, tent-camping in a nearby site, may wish to administer their camp and program through informal cooperative committees, perhaps depending on their pastor as their principal resource person.

A larger group may secure the use of an established camp that already has its own qualified staff for cooking, dishwashing, maintenance of buildings and grounds, and supervision of the waterfront. In such an instance the group would need only provide the program staff for their own activities during its stay at the site. If, however, the group is "on its own," it will need to see that maintenance tasks, meal preparation, cleanup, sanitation, and so on, are provided for.

Let us assume that the staff for the physical plant and functions of the site are provided for in a way that meets the legal requirements and the best standards for such operations and let us turn our attention to the program leadership. There are four basic requirements which should be regarded as absolute minimums for all leadership:

1. An understanding of and commitment to the Christian way of life. Occasionally families of a different faith may be included for some specialized assignment (for example, a Jewish family to help us understand Jewish family life, or a Muslim or a Hindu family to help us understand their cultures) but even in such cases the camp should clearly reflect Christian values and concerns for family relationships.
2. An understanding of the dynamics of family life and the ability to demonstrate those understandings in a relatively successful family. Some single and widowed persons may be engaged for specific assignments.
3. A personal maturity, making it possible to work with others at a deep level with a minimum of friction.
4. A commitment to a philosophy of leadership that believes in persons and seeks to release their potentialities for continual growth.

The leader families in the camping type of experience function largely as resource persons; as expediters helping each family or small group of families to plan, to enjoy, and to grow in a variety of projects such as nature hikes, beach walks, cookouts, out-of-door crafts and through the daily routines of living in the out-of-doors. The leader families are participant members in the group, living with them throughout the duration of the camp; they will help the others gain skill in a variety of activities and share leadership with them. At appropriate times they will also help them gain insight into their family interactions. Basically they will aim to make Christianity a living quality in all activities and relationships.

Leadership for the family camp must be very versatile, combining skills for out-of-door living with real insights in the application of the heritage of the Christian faith to the everyday interactions of daily living within each family. Such leadership is now difficult to find, but we have hopes of developing more of this type through the combined training programs of our denominations and agencies.

At the present time, however, the sponsoring committee should make every effort to secure and, if necessary, provide training experiences for, the best leadership available. Once the sponsoring committee has determined the policies outlined above and the staff has been selected, the director and staff will be responsible for making preparations for the program and guiding the experiences of the camp.

PROGRAM PREPARATIONS

Pre-planning Session

The budget should include provision for the director to assemble the staff families for a day together as soon as the leadership roster is known. Certainly this should be at least a month before the camp, and at the camp site, if at all possible.

After learning about each other's backgrounds and interests, they should get acquainted with the site, either by direct inspection or by having a full description of the facilities and resources with which they will have to work.

Next they should look at the portrait sheets (see Appendix C) of the families enrolled. Families can then be assigned to "colonies," sometimes called "communities." These are groups of three families who will be together throughout the week, sharing in the planning, work, recreation, and worship as a unit.

Families with children about the same age might well be grouped together. Families with younger children should be placed closer to the toilets. New families might well be mixed with more experienced campers, although there are some advantages to a group of new families sharing new experiences together and developing at somewhat the same rate.

If the portrait sheets reveal certain special interests, these might be taken into account when grouping the families into colonies.

Certain activities will usually be coordinated with the total camp group, such as meals, swimming, and evening pow-wows for parents after the children have retired. These can be agreed upon by the leader families working together as a team and in consultation with the manager of the camp property.

The next step is to review the purposes and goals as they have been stated by the sponsoring committee. Perhaps the staff will want to modify or stress some particular aspects of the purpose in the light of the situation in which they will be working or the families which will be attending. The purposes and goals should be so well understood and agreed upon that they become the motivating force for the whole leadership team.

Following the pre-camp planning session, each staff family should begin to assemble resource materials and outline program possibilities. Any supplies should be requisitioned in ample time for delivery to the site. Correspondence might be opened with those families who will be in the colony.

All leader families should plan to arrive on the site the day before the session begins. This will allow time to get comfortably settled and to explore the site if this has not been done before. That evening the leader families can develop the schedule for the first twenty-four hours and check on final details. They also need to have some recreation and worship together. They should be physically rested and spiritually poised to greet the camper families when they arrive.

A Good Beginning

Everything that happens in camp from the moment of arrival until the family departs is part of the program of the camp. The alert staff, therefore, will be "on their toes" (in a relaxed manner, of course!) to provide a good beginning. Some provision will be made to cover the following:

1. A greeter near the entrance to welcome families and to direct them to the registration center (and, if desired, to the toilets)

2. A registration procedure as efficient and expeditious as possible to: (a) assign cabins or suggest tent sites; (b) collect fees, if not previously paid; (c) refer family to health center; (d) perhaps provide a beverage and a cookie

3. Health check by physician or registered nurse. If local regulations do not require a certificate of examination, there should be at least a "3 T Check" on temperature, toes, and throat.

4. Guides to cabins or tent sites. At least one parent of the leader family should be in the colony area to assist families in getting settled. Children may serve as guides. Note: All this may be done on an informal, friendly basis without necessarily labeling the leader family. A community of helpfulness should be developed, but without too much dependence on a designated "leader."

5. Activities. Of course, families will want to get settled. They may be provided with materials to make signs or name tags if they have not made them before. Provision should be made for a refreshing swim and orientation to the aquatic program, or an exploratory tour of the site, if time permits.

The director should "announce" (by poster or mimeo sheet) the evening meal well in advance to give people ample time to find their way to the dining hall. (See dining room suggestions on page 53.)

The first evening's program can be announced at dinner and should be leisurely enough to allow folks weary from traveling to find their way in new surroundings. If an evening vesper is to be a regular feature of the daily schedule, it would be good to introduce it the first evening.

During the remainder of the first evening the colony group may have their own campfire, get acquainted with each other, discuss some of the possibilities of the week.

The next morning after breakfast, worship, and cleanup, the total camp assembles. There can be a get-acquainted session. One device sometimes used here is to have the fathers stand in a circle, with their wives in front of them, and the children in front of the wives according to size. Each family radiates like the spoke of a wheel, and each family can see every other family as a unit.

After the basic structure of the program, such as meal times, swim times, and other total camp activities have been agreed upon, and the necessary work routines and assignments have been established, there can be a general description of some of the possibilities of the week.

Despite the preparatory materials, the director should interpret once more the purpose and spirit of the camp. This should be done with depth of conviction and joyous feeling of adventure in Christian growth. Some of the fathers will surely be skeptical and some of the mothers will be scared. Help them relax in the accepting and supporting atmosphere of Christian fellowship.

Avoid "rules and regulations"—these can be presented informally as the understandings we need to have so that we can all live together in safety and well-being.

Avoid harsh-sounding commands. Instead of "Report at nine o'clock sharp," try using, "Let's gather together as promptly as possible at nine o'clock. We've got a lot of interesting things to do."

Various activities may then be described and any special opportunities in connection with the camp site or the nearby area can be mentioned.

Following this total camp assembly the colony groups can move out together for a more extensive exploration of the camp site. In any hiking or exploratory activity, the colony should move together for two reasons:

as new discoveries are made they can be shared with all of the colony; it also prevents anyone from getting lost.

If the camp is housed in tents, the colony may begin to make plans for improving their tent area. Tables and other conveniences may be useful. These can be constructed out of the materials at hand in good camper fashion.

If the camp is housed in cabins, each colony may want to develop a "home-in-the-woods," where they can meet comfortably and possibly build their own campfire circle and fireplaces for cookouts and such other conveniences as may help them enjoy their time together.

Other special events such as cookouts, tentouts, and hikes may be worked into plans. Special types of collection—rocks, driftwood, and so on, can be considered. Bird watching or star gazing and other special nature interests may also be planned.

It will be impossible to do everything; so the colony will need to begin to select those activities in which they are most interested and to block out their time. Each day they will plan activities for the day. Some time will be devoted to the completion of projects already begun. Other time will be used to start developing activities to satisfy interests not yet met. Always the plans will be kept flexible to meet changing weather conditions and other emerging situations as they arise.

Building their plan day by day, a colony might have a schedule by the end of the week that indicates the use of the major blocks of time each day, as shown in the chart on the next page. This schedule was the creation of one colony. The schedules of other colonies in the same camp varied considerably from this.

Moving On

As the colony begins to roll on its own momentum, the leader families will be especially alert to certain elements in their experiences which they can use to enrich the camp. Many opportunities to observe the dynamics of family interaction will come as parents and their children move from activity to activity throughout the day. Leader families will note the evidences of cooperation, of helpfulness, of support and trust, of forgiveness and love. Some of these can be mentioned in informal conversations, or in the parents' pow-wows around the evening campfires, or perhaps, if appropriate, mentioned in the worship experiences.

	Sunday	Monday	Tuesday	Wednesday	Thursday	Friday	Saturday
MORNING		planning explore site choose home-in-woods	build home-in-woods fireplace	breakfast cookout planning	nature collections	hike lunch-out	community cleanup
AFTERNOON	arrive get settled	rest hour campcraft swim	rest hour finish fireplace swim	rest hour swim prepare campfire for whole camp	rest hour prepare cookout cookout	swim	closing evaluation leave
EVENING	vespers colony campfire	vespers colony campfire	colony vespers and fire	campfire with other colonies	colony vespers games	colony campfire vespers	

Of course, as in any new situation (and in too many old ones) there will be some evidence of tension, pressure, and other less desirable qualities. In one camp a father who was a production engineer was constantly pressuring his son to "get a move on," as they were setting up their tent. Finally the leader asked quietly, "What are you hurrying for? Do you think you're still on the assembly line?" When the father realized his habitual tenseness, you could almost see him begin to "unwind." He was a different man by the end of the week and he and his son were getting along much better.

One of the real opportunities of family camp is to develop better communication between teenagers and adults. By assigning youth to dining room teams and other committees, where they work with adults not their parents, opportunities for new insights can be provided.

As the colony becomes acquainted with the habits of various birds and animals, they will see running through nature many evidences of God's plan and provision for his creatures to have homes and families. Biologists used to think of nature's "law" as the survival of the fittest and poets would claim, "Nature is red in tooth and claw." We now know that there is a delicate and intricate balance in nature and that survival goes to the most cooperative.

When families begin to feel the orderly rhythms, the beauty, and the fundamental goodness of nature, a deeper spirit of serenity and goodness begins to flow through their lives and a new quality is introduced into their patterns of daily living.

Many of these "wonder-full" experiences will provide the natural occasion for worship, and families should be encouraged to express their feelings spontaneously and creatively. Most groups like to have a vesper each evening at which time either the colony or the camp as a whole can lift up in worship some of these experiences. Vespers should be family-planned and directed.

In addition to grace at meals, there should be a time each day when families are encouraged and helped to experiment with their own family devotions. Leaders should see to it that some of the resources of their denomination or some that are listed in the bibliography of this manual are available. Many families trace their observance of family worship to their first experiences in family camp.

As families increase in their awareness of God they will often want to explore his word in the Bible. Some time may be allotted to Bible reading and discussion as a colony in addition to the worship periods.

Music in worship and in general fellowship should be one of the features of camp. It is one of the "naturals" for carry-over value into the home activities of families. Our family has had many happy times and has covered many miles singing the songs we learned in camp.

Music should run like a golden thread throughout the days and activities of camp. Many table graces might be sung. Even the younger children can join in singing graces such as the following (both sung to the tune "Old Hundredth").

Be present at our table, Lord,
Be here and everywhere adored;
These mercies bless, and grant that we
May spend our lives in serving thee.

Lord Jesus, be our holy Guest,
Our morning joy, our evening rest,
And with our daily bread impart
Thy love and peace to every heart.

Other singing in the dining room should be carefully, if subtly, supervised. Loud, boisterous songs have no place at the meal time in a family camp. If some of the quieter fellowship songs are sung it should be after the meal is finished.

There are many other opportunities for music and singing. Work songs can be sung while doing chores. Walking and hiking songs can accompany these activities. Songs from other nations can be real introductions to other cultures. Carefully chosen hymns can enrich vespers. A good camp is a singing camp where music may burst forth spontaneously at any time.

An Effective Closing

As the camp moves toward its conclusion, it should also move toward a climax—a culmination of the spiritual impact on each family. A variety of programs have been used and new variations and combinations are constantly tried. Some effective programs have been:

1. *A Fellowship Circle.* This circle, long familiar in youth camps, is appropriately used with a variation for the family camp. The members of each family join hands, making a small circle. Each family circle links up with the two circles next to them, making the larger circle a chain of family links.

At first each family faces inward on itself, thanking God for the experiences of the camp. Then they face outward, pledging themselves in service to others and to Christ's kingdom. Prayers may be interspersed with hymns that have become meaningful during the camp.

Such a circle makes an effective closing after the last meal, just before departure. Remember the children; don't make it too long-drawn-out.

If families have been saving their money during the camp for some gift of sharing, they may bring their gifts at the closing circle.

In some camps spokesmen for each family have made brief statements about their family goals growing out of the camp experience.

2. *Closing Worship.* Sometimes the closing evening's vesper service has been made the high point of the camp.

In other camps, the adults have had a special closing worship at the end of the last evening of camp. In one camp where the conditions and spirit seemed just right, the camp pastor led the adult couples in a rededication to their marriage vows. This, however, must be carefully handled. It is awkward if there are any widowed or divorced parents present. And the rededication, if used, should avoid any forced or sticky sentimentalisms. Far better a simple service of prayer for the benediction of the camp.

3. *Camp Covenants.* Many camps have felt a value in suggesting that families set down in permanent form some of the high resolutions that grow out of the camp experience. This has been done in various ways, such as: (a) a statement formulated by a representative committee gathering up some of the great themes of the experience together (see Appendix F); (b) some families have written themselves letters which were left with the camp director who mailed them about January 1 of the following year; (c) other families have simply written out the statement they agreed upon for the closing fellowship circle and have kept it as part of their own camp mementos.

However it is done, some opportunity should be given to families to think clearly about the implications of the kind of living they have experienced in family camp for their daily living at home, and they should be encouraged to plan some practical next steps to carry the values of the camp experience back into their homes. Whether or not any public record is kept or word expressed, they should be encouraged to acknowledge that the experiences of camp were a reality and a clue to what might become real in their own home life.

An Evaluation and Follow-up

While the experience is fresh it is also good to get some evaluation of the experience to guide the sponsoring committee and staff in making plans for future camps.

One camp hands a sheet to each family at the last evening meal. They are encouraged to discuss it in their family session before vespers and to answer the simple questions (see below). This blank must be handed to the director at the gate as they leave. He calls it their "passport" back to civilization.

The evaluation blank need not be complicated. Questions like the following may be used:

What did you (like most) (find most helpful) about camp?

What suggestions do you have for our next camp? (This can be open, or it might specify suggestions for program, leaders, dining hall, food service, and so on.)

More elaborate check lists might be used with ratings for various aspects of the program, but these are seldom necessary. Campers are usually a very outspoken lot!

Be sure that children's evaluative comments are included in the written responses. These can be very enlightening.

Some camps have an assembly where the campers can share what the camp has meant to them along with their suggestions for future camps. Where this is done, it needs skillful handling to avoid becoming a "gripe" session on the one hand or a self-congratulatory adulation on the other.

On the whole, a simple, written response usually provides more thoughtful objectivity.

An evaluation session by the leader families is of great value. If it can be arranged for them to stay over for a period after the campers leave, they can give their own evaluations while they are fresh. After this is done, a review of the campers' recommendations may be made. Recommendations to the sponsoring committee can grow out of the staff and camper evaluations. This should be done promptly to help the sponsoring committee in its planning for the following year.

Many camps have had a follow-up in the form of a reunion in the fall following a summer camp, especially if the camp is sponsored by an area presbytery, district, or conference. Such a reunion is usually spontaneously suggested by campers who feel "we must get together sometime!" A reunion has a two-fold advantage: (1) it provides another type of evaluation by the very attendance and the reminiscences, and (2) it helps in promoting interest in future camps.

A reunion may be simply arranged. A centrally located church can invite the group in the fall. The campers may bring their lunches or they may be served a meal at cost if advance reservations are made.

Usually they come to the Sunday morning worship service of the host church. After lunch they show snaps or slides of the preceding summer's camp and report on some of the things the families have been doing or thinking since summer. Camp songs may be sung and a brief camp-style worship service may conclude the afternoon's fellowship—early enough to let the families get home by bedtime.

If the sponsoring committee can announce the dates and the leadership for the next camps, that helps to increase the momentum of the interest of the campers.

Caution: It is inadvisable to allow visitors or "prospects" for future camps to attend a reunion. This changes the "reunion" into some kind of camp promotion scheme, with results that are quite different.

Where a camp reunion does not seem feasible, families within traveling distance may be encouraged to visit each other.

THE FAMILY CONFERENCE

THREE: PLANNING A FAMILY CONFERENCE

PURPOSES AND GOALS

A family conference is somewhat like a honeymoon. It is an experience in a new setting, free from accustomed responsibilities and routines, during which the persons involved can devote their time and attention to establishing newer and more satisfying relationships in the light of their Christian commitment.

Unlike the honeymoon, however, the family conference involves a group of families living, working, studying, playing, and worshiping together in a common quest to understand more fully and to demonstrate more clearly the power of Christ in their family living.

To attempt to gather these thoughts in a more precise definition, we might say: "A Christian family conference is an experience of living in a community designed to help each family respond increasingly to God's love as revealed in Christ. Through shared work, study, play, and worship, and with the guiding and supporting fellowship of the church, the participating families seek to grow in the understanding and practice of Christian love."

The sponsoring committee will need to make its decisions in the light of its own purposes and with due consideration of the needs and readiness of its families. If it decides on a conference experience, the committee will need to locate an adequate site.

STANDARDS

Site, Facilities, and Equipment

A conference, like a honeymoon, will probably be helped by beautiful natural surroundings. If the committee is inclined to consider a camp site for its conference, it will want to be sure to read what was said about sites in the preceding chapter on camping.

A conference, however, may meet at a resort hotel, or a college campus or some other similar conference center. In either event, the committee will find the check list in Appendix A helpful.

Duration, Size, and Cost

In any educational or growth experience, the length of time is an important factor. A local congregation, whose families already are well acquainted, can sponsor a well-planned weekend that will be a very rewarding experience. A full week together would multiply the benefits.

Conferences sponsored by some synod, diocese, or other area organization, which bring strangers together should consider five days a minimum. A full seven-day week would be better. Some conferences are planned for ten days or two weeks.

A local church could sponsor a weekend conference with three or more of its families. One church reserved all the rooms of a motel during an off-season weekend, and held their discussions in the parish house of a nearby church. On Sunday morning they joined with the local congregation in worship.

Many facilities can accommodate thirty, fifty, or even more families and it is always a temptation to try to bring together the largest group possible both for reasons of economy and eagerness to reach as many families as possible. We were in a conference once that enrolled fifty families, totaling over 160 persons. While the conference was not without some value for those who attended, the large numbers tended to overstimulate the children. The teenagers tended to gang up and go off on their own. Even the parents tended to fragment into a number of small groups, usually based on their friendships prior to camp. This tendency toward cliquishness left out some of the newcomers and impaired the movement of the whole group toward unity.

Our present knowledge of sound educational procedures and our experience with groups would indicate that a group of twenty families should be considered maximum. This would mean a total of between eighty to one hundred persons. To exceed this maximum would create problems that even the most careful planning could not eliminate.

It should be firmly stressed, however, that all members normally residing in the household should participate in the conference. This includes grandparents or maiden aunts who may be living in the home. If the conference is to lift the level of family living, this can happen much more readily when all who live together share in the experience.

It is important that the age of all who attend should be such that they are not too much of a burden on the other members of the family. Experience indicates that children under four should not be included in the family conference. Their participation is limited and they limit participation of other members of the family. This policy should be clearly announced in all presentations or publicity so that there will be no misunderstanding.

Financing a family conference will need the careful attention of the sponsoring committee. Because of each family's need for privacy, living accommodations usually cannot be filled as efficiently as when occupied by sex-segregated groups. Economic considerations should never be allowed to destroy privacy.

If the sponsoring agency is convinced of the value of this kind of experience it will also make sure that any family, regardless of its size, is able to take advantage of it. Many conferences have established a "family rate" of about $65 to $75 per week regardless of the size of the family. This tends to insure the attendance by the total family unit.

Some conferences have a sliding scale of fees graduated according to adults, teenagers, and children under twelve. Others use a consumer cooperative plan, charging a fixed fee for certain fixed costs, then sharing only the actual costs of food and other supplies.

Local churches may use some of their education budget, or special funds, to provide leadership for their conference, leaving the families to cover the living expenses. Congregations often share in the costs of sending their families to conferences sponsored by synods, districts, or other denominational agencies.

Careful financial records should be kept and sound procedures followed regarding purchases and payments for expenses. Some type of insurance coverage should be arranged. Agreements with site managements, staff, and any related personnel should be in writing.

Staff Personnel

Depending on the size and location of the conference, staff requirements will vary greatly. Three or four families from a local congregation may wish to administer their conference through informal cooperative committees, perhaps depending on their pastor as their principal resource person.

The quarters for larger conferences usually have their own qualified staff for cooking, dishwashing, maintenance of buildings and grounds, and supervision of the waterfront. In such an instance this group would need only to provide the program staff for their own activities during their stay at the site.

Let us assume that the staff for the physical plant and functions of the site are provided for in a way that meets the legal requirements and the best standards for such operations and let us turn our attention to the program leadership.

The four requirements we listed as basic for camp leadership on page 33, also apply to conference leadership.
Briefly stated they are:

1. An understanding of and commitment to the Christian life
2. An understanding of the dynamics of family interaction
3. A personal maturity and ability to work with others
4. A commitment to shared leadership that releases the potentialities for continual growth and leadership in others.

The leader of the conference has a basic concern to see that Christianity becomes a living quality in all of the activities and relationships within the family. In the conference type of program, however, he will function somewhat more like a teacher. Of course the leader's family will share as a participant in all of the activities of the conference, but his leadership is more apt to be in a particular area of pre-assigned responsibility. He may be responsible for leading the parent discussions on family relationships, or the activities for children or youth during designated periods.

The program staff of a family conference can be kept to a modest number. Many responsibilities can be carried forward by families or committees, reducing the need for invited staff. When leader families are invited, often the different members can carry different specific responsibilities in accordance with their talents. For example, a father may lead the children's activities, the mother may lead the parent discussions, while a son can coordinate the craft activities.

The following functions or areas of responsibility will need to be provided either by staff invited for the specific purpose, by designated families from among those planning to attend, or by committees made up of individual members of several families:

1. *General Administration.* Co-directors, usually a lay couple, have general oversight and administration of the total program. It is preferable to avoid the academic formality suggested by the title "dean."

2. *Worship.* This is usually planned by a committee. The pastor or some clergyman may be invited to bring the vesper messages, but he should involve others in the conduct of the services. This committee is also responsible for arranging grace at meals, and making suggestions for individual family worship.

3. *Discussions for Parents.* Such discussions may be organized by a committee, but more frequently they are assigned to a specially invited resource leader.

4. *Activities for Children and Youth.* When age-segregated activities seem desirable, leadership may need to be provided at several levels, according to age distribution. (See activity suggestions on page 59.) Usually such activities are directed by invited leadership.

5. *Hobbies and Crafts.* Usually these are coordinated by one person, assisted by various delegates who share their skills with others. If the conference is in an out-of-door setting, nature appreciation and some skills in out-of-door living may be included in these activities.

6. *Music.* One or more delegates may have responsibility for leading the singing for fellowship and worship.

7. *Recreational Activities.* Usually organized by committees of conferences according to their interests.

It is also desirable to arrange for the attendance of a family representing another nationality or race, or a missionary family, who can help the other families appreciate the wider horizons of the Christian experience.

It is the function of the sponsoring committee to see that leadership for these functions is the best possible. It should feel a responsibility for making training experience available to potential leaders.

Once the sponsoring committee has determined the policies outlined above and the staff has been selected, the co-directors and the staff will be responsible for planning the program of the conference.

PROGRAM PLANNING

Pre-planning Session

The budget should include provision for the co-directors to assemble the staff families for a day together as soon as the leadership roster is known. Certainly this should be at least a month before the conference, and on the grounds if at all possible. This pre-planning session is in addition to the fact that the staff families should arrive on the site twenty-four hours before the conference begins.

After learning each other's backgrounds and their assigned responsibilities, they should get acquainted with the facilities in which they will be working, either by direct inspection or by having a detailed description.

Next they should look at the portrait sheets (see Appendix C) of the families enrolled. If any special interests or circumstances are revealed, these should be carefully noted.

Living accommodations can be assigned by the co-directors, keeping the families with younger children closer to the toilets and mixing new families among those with previous experience.

The next step is to review the purposes and goals as they have been stated by the sponsoring committee. Perhaps the staff will want to modify or stress some particular aspects of the purpose in the light of the situation in which they will be working or the families which will be attending. The purposes and goals should be so well understood and agreed upon that they become the motivating force for the whole leadership team.

The staff can then begin to build the various elements of a conference experience into the program. Of course, everything that happens, from the moment of arrival until the family departs for home is (or should be!) part of the learning and growing of the conference experience. For convenience, however, we can identify the following elements.

A Good Beginning

Plans will need to be made for the following:

1. A greeter near the entrance to welcome families and to direct them to the registration center (and, if desired, to the toilets)
2. A registration procedure as efficient and expeditious as possible to:

(a) assign living accommodations; (b) collect fees; (c) refer family to health center; (d) perhaps provide a beverage and a cookie

3. Health check by physician or registered nurse. If local regulations do not require a certificate or examination, there should at least be a "3 T Check" on temperature, toes, and throat.

4. Guides to living quarters. Often children of staff families like this assignment.

5. Activities. Of course families will want to get settled. They may be provided with materials to make signs and name tags if they have not made them before.

A supervised play area might be provided for little ones while the parents are getting settled.

Provision should be made for swimming, or an exploratory tour of the grounds, if time permits.

The director should plan to tell the families about the first meal well in advance in order to give them ample time to find their way to the dining hall.

Dining Room Suggestions

There should be a hostess-supervisor in the dining hall. The co-director wife will often handle this as part of the over-all conference administration.

At many conference centers the conferees have only to set the tables, serve the food from a counter to the tables, and clear the tables following the meal.

The hostess will organize the teams of servers. Sometimes the various teams will each serve one meal in turn. Other conferences have each team serve the three meals for one day. Teams are made up of one member from each family up to the number required to provide a server for each table. Each team usually has a leader who acts as the hostess-supervisor for that meal.

Seating is very important in a family conference. If there is no plan, families with small children often get separated and there is general confusion and scrambling for seats.

One plan that has worked well is for the hostess to prepare a large name card for each family and indicate on it the number in the family and the number of children needing "assist" chairs. She then works out the combinations of families that will fill each table. Tables should not have more than eight places. By placing the cards on the tables the waiters know how to set them. When the families arrive they can look for their place cards, knowing they will all be able to sit together without a breathless scramble. By shifting the combinations various families can get acquainted. Some conferences like to shift each meal (which usually means that the same combinations will sit together several times during the week). Others like to let the same combination sit together a day at a time.

Sometimes at luncheon, all the teenagers might be allowed to sit at special tables.

If the management of the conference center likes to place the dessert on the table at the beginning of the meal, they should be reminded that with younger children attending, this should be avoided.

The atmosphere in the dining room should be kept quietly relaxing and care should be taken that younger children do not get overstimulated at meal time. Children seven and over can be assigned to waiter teams as helpers—with due care taken about their handling of heavy or hot serving dishes. It must be made clear, however, that only the serving team should move about during the meal. Otherwise this can create considerable confusion.

If songs are sung, they should be of the quieter type and should not begin until the tables are cleared. Announcements should be kept to a minimum.

The First Meeting

The first meeting is very important in setting the mood for the week. Depending on when the conference begins, it may be planned for the afternoon or the evening. Some simple get-acquainted mixers are desirable as soon as the families begin to assemble. When most of the group have arrived, some group singing is always appropriate. Then it might be well to give the whole group a chance to introduce themselves as families, giving the names and ages of the children.

Care should be taken during this get-acquainted time to avoid status symbols. Leave off titles and do not ask for occupations. Let plumbers and bankers, farmers and lawyers, mix without labels. When in the course of the conference they do discover what each does, they may be in for some wonderful surprises.

Despite the preparatory materials, the directors should interpret once more the purpose and spirit of the conference. This should be done with depth of conviction and a joyous feeling of adventure in Christian growth. Some of the fathers will surely be skeptical and some of the mothers will be scared. Help them to relax in the accepting and supporting atmosphere of Christian fellowship.

Avoid "rules and regulations"—these can be presented informally as the understandings we need to have so that we can all live together in safety and well-being.

Avoid harsh sounding commands. Instead of "Report for classes at nine o'clock sharp," try using, "Let's gather together as promptly as possible at nine o'clock. We've got a lot of interesting things to talk over."

Draw the families together with a contagious enthusiasm rather than by the exercise of authority. In most of the conferences in which the authors participate, we make it quite clear that only one thing is "required"—conferees do not have to come to meals, but they *must* observe the rest hour after lunch. Then we tell them about the father who resented this requirement and grumblingly stretched out on his bed "just until the kids get to sleep." After the youngsters and their mother came back from swimming late in the afternoon, they woke him to get ready for supper. (Fathers often need this kind of suggestion to help them "unwind" after the pressures of business.)

Then the program can be reviewed and schedules distributed if they have not been sent in advance. Any necessary work routines and assignments can be established at this meeting.

Have the first meeting well planned so that there will be no fumbling around or lost motion, yet make it look as relaxed as a leisurely conversation. Give folks the idea that something real is going to happen every day of the conference, and they will not want to miss a session.

If it is an evening session, it would be good to bring it to a close with an informal period of "coffee, cocoa, and conversation." Some of the most valuable sharing of experiences comes during these evening snacks.

In family conferences there need not be a formal "lights out" time, but everyone should be encouraged to get adequate rest for the full day ahead.

The Over-all Schedule

The staff will then proceed to work out the proposed schedule for the conference. This will be subject to review and adaptation by the conference council and it may be changed or varied as the activities progress. Such a schedule might look somewhat as follows:

7:00 a.m.	Rising
7:45 a.m.	Breakfast (morning devotions at table)
8:30 a.m.	Housekeeping
9:15 a.m.	Age-level activities for children
9:15 a.m.	Parents' Bible study or chaplain's hour
10:00 a.m.	Parents' discussion of Christian family life
11:00 a.m.	Family hour: hike, swim, projects
12:15 p.m.	Luncheon
1:00 p.m.	Rest Hour
2:00 p.m.	Quiet projects, crafts, etc., for those awake
3:00 p.m.	Family hobbies, sports, swimming, etc.
5:45 p.m.	Dinner
6:30 p.m.	Family fun and informal games
7:15 p.m.	Individual family worship
7:30 p.m.	Vespers
8:15 p.m.	Bedtime (for juniors and younger)
8:45 p.m.	Parents' evening program (teenagers with parents or in own group)
10:00 p.m.	Fellowship snack (coffee, cocoa, and conversation)

Basic Principles of Scheduling

Keep the schedule leisurely:

–toddlers take time

–housekeeping by families takes time

–besides, it's vacation!

After-dinner activities may be adjusted in order to take advantage of sunset at vesper time.

Regional variations should be kept in mind (for example, in the warm southwest, hikes and other physical activities were scheduled in the cool of the morning).

Keep all schedules flexible enough to meet changing circumstances (such as weather) and interests of the group.

Parent Discussions

The staff will want to plan some opportunities for the parents to think together about Christian family life and nurture in the home. These may be provided by having age-segregated periods during the morning, as in the schedule given earlier, or by having the planned discussions in the evening after the younger children have gone to bed. Evening sessions have the advantage of allowing the parents to be with their children throughout the day, but they have a disadvantage in that the parents are rather weary by the close of the day.

Even when there are morning sessions for parents, sometimes one or two evenings are given over to the presentation of movies or plays dealing with family situations. These can be discussed over the coffee or cocoa until bedtime.

One of the real opportunities of a family conference is to develop better communication between teenagers and their parents. By assigning youth to dining room teams and to other committees (sometimes even asking them to be chairman), where they work with adults not their parents, opportunities for new insights can be provided. An excellent morning or evening discussion can be developed with both teenagers and adults in the same session. An excellent way is to show a family movie or read a play and then divide the teenagers into small groups with adults, not their parents, to discuss it. Many parents have confessed to the value of such a discussion with teenagers when they were not emotionally involved as a parent.

Other topics that frequently recur in the interests of parents are: discipline, understanding child development, resisting community pressures, developing community responsibility, handling hostilities, wise use of time and money.

Many of these lead right into questions of choice and the moral basis on which we make choices. Matters of faith are directly involved, therefore ample time must also be allowed for the specific discussion of faith. This may be done by scheduling a special period to deal with Bible study or questions of a more specific religious nature. Some conferences work this material in with the other developmental questions, using the same leadership. Other conferences may develop a dialogue between a family life consultant and a clergyman, each bringing out their respective aspects of the same questions.

The number and variety of youth activities at the family conference will be planned in accordance with the number in that age category who are present. All sons and daughters older than high school should participate in the adult discussions. If there are fewer than eight of high school age, they too can be readily absorbed into the adult discussions.

If there are about ten or more young people who are in the 7th to 12th grades at school, the staff should consider whether it would be wise to plan for some special activities for this age group.

A leader should be provided for the youth fellowship who can meet with them while the parents are having their discussions. He can use some of the youth responses on the Portrait Sheets (see Appendix C) as his starting point. Young people of this age are often interested in vocational choices and the inspirational character of the family conference is a good background against which to consider such choices.

If there is a family of another race or nationality in the conference, they may be invited to meet with the youth for a session or two.

The youth leader should keep in touch with the leader of the parent discussions and when both groups are ready they might merge for one or more sessions to discuss the relations of teenagers with their parents.

During the evening discussions the youth might well be mixed with the parents. They may, however, prefer to spend one or two of their evenings pursuing their own interests.

It is always good if one leader can meet with the youth throughout all of their separate sessions, even though other guests may be invited to speak on certain topics. The continuous leadership develops a rapport with the young people and the leader is better able to develop an experience of growth as well as experiences of understanding and communication with parents.

Certainly teenagers should be appointed along with adults to all of the work teams and conference committees. This shared responsibility for the total conference enterprise is most valuable.

Occasionally the youth fellowship as a unit will undertake some responsibility on behalf of the total conference. They may, for instance, work with the waterfront director in organizing and conducting a water carnival for the conference, or plan some other kind of recreational event. They may also help to conduct one of the vesper services.

The major emphasis should be on participation in the family activities of the conference. The youth fellowship should not become self-conscious or overactive to the point where its activities interfere with the total family activities.

Children's Activities

The conference staff will also need to plan the activities for the various age groups of children for that portion of each day when age-segregated activities seem appropriate. Some folks are so family-centered in their thinking that they regard any age-segregated activity as a violation of the spirit of family programs. Anyone who has ever lived in a family, however, knows that there are certain times of every day when adults pursue their interests while the children play with those of their own age. This rhythm of activities for children and youth does not seem to us to violate the spirit of family living which recognizes the developmental needs of the various members, as long as the major portion of the day's program offers activities to the family as a unit.

Since, in the conference setting, you cannot simply send the children "out to play," and since the age-segregated activities also provide a valuable opportunity for helping the various age groups "respond increasingly to God's love as revealed in Christ," activities ought to be carefully planned as a vital part of the total conference experience.

The variety of activities that could be done with boys and girls depends on the amount of time at your disposal and on the setting for the conference. If there is a two-hour session in the morning, it can be broken into periods for some discussion, some project activity, some recreation, and some worship.

If a theme for the week is selected, it will help the children to tie together their experiences. A leader for each age group, qualified and experienced in working with children, should be designated. An assortment of books on various topics can be made available for children to use during their quiet hours. It is always wise to have some movies on hand—particularly those dealing with animals and wildlife—to use especially if the weather prevents outdoor activity.

If the conference is held on a site where some nature study is possible, the interest in the out-of-doors and in families can often be merged into a series of activities for junior-age youngsters such as the following. The theme used here is "God Has Provided Homes."

SESSION 1

TOPIC: How God's plan provides a home for every living thing—a home best suited for its needs

DISCUSSION: After getting acquainted with the boys and girls, discuss the various kinds of homes we know about.

ACTIVITY: After discussion and browsing through some books, decide on some animal for special study. The study may include: (1) making a diorama of the home of an animal; (2) making a three dimensional picture showing the cross section of a home such as a beehive, wasp nest, or beaver dam.

RESOURCES: The University of Chicago Basic Science Education Series. (Inexpensive books with excellent drawings and pictures of insects, animals, fish, and so on). Row, Peterson & Co., Evanston, Ill.

The Golden Book of Nature Crafts, by John Saunders. Golden Press, 1958.

Secrets by Jessie Orton Jones. Viking Press, 1945.

SESSION 2

TOPIC: Different Kinds of Homes

DISCUSSION: What different kinds of homes do living things have?

ACTIVITY: Take a walk and write down the homes we see (it is well to have at least one magnifying glass for each four children). After walk, compare notes and make a composite list (using flow pen on large sheet of paper). Also start gathering materials for major project.

SESSION 3

TOPIC: Adaptation to Environment

ACTIVITY—Discussion: Have children bring to group anything they have caught (frogs, worms, insects, etc.). Discuss how to care for these until they are returned to their homes at the end of the session. Study adaptive device, webbed feet, gills, eyelids, and so on. List on large sheet, "Things I Learned Today."

SESSION 4

TOPIC: Protection Afforded by Homes

DISCUSSION: How do various types of homes provide protection and suitable environment for young until they can take care of themselves?

ACTIVITY: Work on major project selected during first session.

Session 5

Topic: Homes for Growth According to God's Plan

Discussion: Reports describing homes built, and how they provide for security and growth of its inhabitants

Activity: Compose, as a group, a litany of thanks to God for all the homes in this world.

Arrange for an "open house" so others can see all the group has discovered.

Throughout all these discussions, parallels can be drawn with the care, protection, and nurture of human families and insights can be gained for mutual helpfulness in the home. For younger children of the primary age a similar series of sessions could be developed out of the daily vacation Bible school text, *The Earth Is Full of Thy Riches,* stressing how all living things grow according to God's pattern.

Family Activities

The conference staff will allow the major portion of each day for activity by families. In addition to eating and sleeping, there will be adventures in worship, crafts, recreation, discussion, and decision-making. While the initiative and integrity of each family needs to be respected, the staff will need to provide leadership and supervision for some activities such as swimming, while for others the staff will need to provide resources to assist families, as in learning new crafts.

In the schedule suggested earlier, it will be noted that the eleven o'clock hour in the morning is a family hour. Swimming is usually the principal activity of this hour, although some families will take walks or spend their time in other ways as they choose. Usually there are no special offerings of crafts or games at this morning hour since the families are encouraged to function on their own initiative as units.

The afternoon, following the lunch and rest hours, should be kept perfectly free for families to engage in whatever activities they wish. If the activity area is close to the sleeping area, the activities from two o'clock until two-thirty or three may be restricted to the quieter crafts in order that the younger children may enjoy longer naps. Some conferences call this the "tiptoe hour."

Crafts. One of the prime purposes of the family conference is to knit the family together with an increasing number of activities they enjoy doing together. If the conference is in an out-of-door setting, nature study, crafts, and collections would be a "natural." It is also valid to help the families gain some skills in crafts they can share together in the home throughout the year. Jewelry making, copper enameling, aluminum craft, leatherwork, and a host of other craft hobbies can be introduced to families.

Some conferences insist that at least one parent work with each child on a craft so that it becomes a shared skill or interest in the home. If the whole family can agree to explore and develop a craft together, so much the better (and the process of decision-making may prove to be the most valuable part of the whole experience).

The conference staff will designate a craft coordinator. He can use the portrait sheets to determine those crafts in which there is most interest and also whether there are among the conference families some who are willing to take the leadership in sharing a craft with the rest of the group. It helps to suggest that a leader share his hobby for only two or three days, so that he can use the remaining days to be free to explore new crafts with his own family.

The craft coordinator should be responsible for ordering all of the necessary craft supplies. He may ask various families to bring the supplies for their specialty, but he should advise as to probable demand to keep the costs of supplies within budget limitations.

In planning for crafts, it is good to offer some simple things in which the younger children can share as well as those requiring more skill for more advanced persons. Something like clay modeling using a pottery clay that needs no firing, can be used by children, but also worked into more elaborate forms by adults.

Leatherworking also may begin with simple "do-it-yourself" kits which give youngsters some real satisfaction, but might also include some advanced tooling designs for those with more experience in leatherwork.

Emphasis should be on the enjoyment of self-expression and shared enthusiasms, rather than on technical perfection. Any exhibits should include the work of all, including the youngest. Do we need to add that there should be no competition or prizes?

Recreation. While recreational activities will usually be under the direction of a committee of the conferees, the staff will want to do some advance planning to insure adequate use of the facilities of the conference site, and that the necessary equipment is available.

The emphasis should be on the more simple and less expensive forms of recreation which families can enjoy together, such as hiking, swimming, and so on. Sometimes segments of families may enjoy a sport together, as when father and son comprise a doubles team for tennis, or when husband and wife pair off for badminton (parents have a right to enjoy themselves together!).

Sports in which only one member of the family is active should not be given any time in the family conference schedule. Elaborate tournaments and competitions are to be avoided. In one conference, two fathers played off the ping-pong singles championship at 1:30 a.m. of the closing day of camp. This kind of build-up of pressure in the schedule is inexcusable.

Spectator sports should be avoided. This may be difficult because of the widespread tendency toward this type of activity. Many parents actually must be taught how to *play with* their children. Left to their own devices, they may never adopt a family hobby or learn any new skills together, or enter into family games. The recreation program at a family conference is, therefore, a serious matter. Through it families learn techniques and resources to carry over into their home life.

Play activity is important for another reason. A family conference is usually a vacation time for most of the families. It ought to feel like a vacation, with plenty of fun and relaxation. Experience indicates that it is unwise to shortchange this fun feature.

Those who lead the recreation should be skillful and patient in helping grownups and children play together. Simple rhythmic games and folk dances with songs that accompany them are fun for most families.

Swimming should be available in summer family conferences if at all possible. The recreation committee should have a subcommittee to help the waterfront director, but each family should be charged with the primary responsibility for its own members.

If there is to be instruction given in swimming or other skills, it is always better if parents can be helped to teach their own children. Any approach that helps build the ties between parents and their children should be explored.

"Talent" nights are questionable if they tend to show off only one member of a family. It is better to have a "Family Fun Night" stressing the participation of all family members.

Caution should be exercised in the development of the recreation program. It is not wise to pack into one week all the games and sports a committee can think of. Families should not return home worn out. It is especially important to avoid overstimulation of children. Recreation should always be regarded as a means toward Christian fellowship and not an end in itself.

Music. Music has one of the greatest possibilities for carry-over value into the home activities of families. Our family has had many happy times and has covered many miles singing the songs we learned in family conferences.

Music should run like a golden thread throughout the days and activities of the conference. The first song in the morning might well be a hymn of praise played on a trumpet or over a loud-speaker.

Many table graces might be sung. Even the younger children can join in singing graces such as the following, sung to the tune "Old Hundredth."

> Lord, gratitude we offer all,
> Who labor that we may be fed;
> O bless us as we work for them,
> Bring kinship through our daily bread.*

Other singing in the dining room should be carefully, if subtly, supervised. Loud, boisterous songs have no place at meal time. If some of the quieter fellowship songs are sung, it should be after the meal is finished and the tables have been cleared.

There are many other opportunities for music and singing. Work songs can be sung while doing chores. Walking and hiking songs can accompany these activities. Songs from other nations can be a real introduction to other cultures. Carefully chosen hymns can enrich the vespers.

A good conference is a singing conference where music may burst forth spontaneously at any time.

Worship. During the family conference many families will begin experimenting with new forms and ideas of family worship (many for the first time!). In addition to the opportunities offered by the conference schedule, the staff will want to plan for adequate resources and for some guidance to assist those families that want help.

Denominations that use liturgical forms of worship will find the family conference an excellent opportunity to acquaint families with their forms

* See other grace suggestions on pages 39 and 40.

for family worship and to enrich their understanding of the stated hours for daily observance.

In addition to the corporate experiences of worship for all the families at the conference, there should be opportunities and encouragement for individual families to worship as units. In many conferences, if there are sound amplification facilities, a family may conduct table devotions in a way that is genuine worship in its own right, but also serves as an example of what might be done by other families.

The early morning watch, so popular in youth conferences, is hardly applicable to the family camp because of the younger children. The children do not prevent some conferences, however, from scheduling a period of meditation during which families can begin the day with prayer together.

By far the most popular time is the vesper after the evening meal. This can be either the highest point or the lowest point of the day. In far too many cases it is the latter. When the service is too long, too dreary, does not communicate, it is indeed unfortunate because it is not only unpleasant but it also teaches all the families that corporate worship by families is something to be avoided.

The conference staff should plan to work with a worship committee of the conferees to see that the services are brief, resourceful, and with real meaning to the whole family. The leadership of the services should include campers of various ages who can read scripture and lead in prayer. Simple music, rightly used, can enrich the services.

One of the most effective series of vespers related each service to the period of individual family worship which immediately preceded the vesper. At the close of dinner each evening, a text or a question was given for the families to consider in their devotional period. As the families gathered for worship in their cabins or out under a tree, they discussed this question and then moved directly to the vesper where the question or text was developed more fully.

Many staffs have found it valuable to prepare a mimeographed guide for the period of individual family worship. Denominational family devotional guides or "A Week of Family Devotions" published by the National Council of Churches are often selected. Families usually need some specific helps to get started in this practice that is new to most of them.

Table grace is another place where many families need help. Many conferences provide for each meal a little card on which is printed a grace that can be read or sung together. At the close of the conference, each family is given a packet of these cards to take home.

The Sunday morning worship service in a family camp differs little from the vespers, except that it may include a special offering for some cause selected by the families, and perhaps it may include some special music. The important factor is that all the family can worship together regardless of their ages. For this reason the service should be brief and interesting, even to the younger children.

An Effective Closing

The suggestions made in the preceding chapter regarding family camps (page 40) are also appropriate for family conferences. The conference staff should begin in the earliest planning to consider toward what kind of climax they wish to move. Although this may be modified during the course of the conference it will be valuable in providing a sense of direction.

An Evaluation and Follow-up

The conference staff should plan from the beginning for some kind of evaluation and follow-up. The simple evaluation suggested in the preceding chapter on family camps can easily be adapted to the goals of a family conference. The suggestions regarding follow-up are also applicable to a family conference.

* * * *

By the close of the planning session, the staff families should have an understanding of each other and of the specific responsibilities and be ready to function as a team—one for all and all for one—as they carry forward the program.

Following the program planning session, each staff family should begin to assemble their resource materials and develop more detailed program plans. Any supplies should be requisitioned in ample time for delivery at the conference. Correspondence should be opened with those families who might be asked to assume special leadership responsibilities.

All staff families should plan to arrive on the site the day before the conference begins. This will allow time to get settled and to explore the facilities if this has not been done before. That evening the staff families can check on final details and also have some recreation and worship together. They should be physically rested and spiritually poised to greet the camper families as they arrive.

Once the conference is under way, the plans described earlier can be carried out. It is valuable for the leadership staff and the committee chairmen to meet briefly each day to coordinate plans as they are developed by the committees and to modify previously made plans as may be necessary.

In some conferences, the co-directors will create a family council composed of one member from each family. (In one it was suggested that each family with children over twelve send the child who was closest to twelve years of age. Families whose oldest child was younger than twelve were asked to send either the husband or the wife. By this plan the council represented a cross section of age and sex as well as each family in the conference.) The council receives the suggested schedule and activities from the staff and committees and acts upon them. The council can also initiate its own ideas for the good of the conference. Each council member is encouraged to discuss the ideas with his own family. This stimulates the processes of discussion and decision-making within each family.

FOUR: AREAS OF CONCERN AND OPPORTUNITY

SERVING FAMILIES WITH SPECIAL NEEDS

In any congregation there are families with special needs—the widowed, the orphaned, the physically and mentally handicapped. The ministry and fellowship of the church must embrace and sustain them in the name of our God who loves the last, the least, and the least attractive. Family life committees should be especially alert to make sure that these families also have some opportunities for appropriate camp or conference experiences.

Committees serving metropolitan or state areas may discover enough families with the same needs so that it would be wise to provide special camps or conferences especially designed for these families.

If there are not sufficient numbers to justify such a special opportunity, these families will have to be included with groups of regular families. There are many advantages to this plan, because often the thing such families need most is a loving, accepting, meaningful association with average families. However, to incorporate certain types of families into an ongoing camp or conference requires a special alertness on the part of leadership and a quality of concern in the conduct of the program.

It must also be frankly and honestly recognized that it would be unwise for certain families, for instance those with certain types of handicapped children, to attempt to participate in some kinds of camp or conference experiences.

As of this writing, experiments have not been conducted on which to base firm recommendations for "special need" families. Resourceful and imaginative families are finding that in many activities they can go far beyond the limits they originally anticipated. It is the responsibility of our churches and agencies to stimulate, encourage, and support these explorations and to help these families grow in self-reliance and the fullness of life as they respond to God's love.

Parents Without Partners

Within the last five years a nationwide association of fathers and mothers who are rearing their children without a partner has developed. Many of the local chapters of this organization have been initiated or aided by church leaders. They have sponsored some excellent conventions and conferences and they are now beginning to experiment with family camps. Further information can be secured from Parents Without Partners, Inc., 80 Fifth Avenue, New York, N. Y.

Most fathers or mothers who are trying to go it alone have developed a self-reliant attitude. Some who have been recently bereaved or divorced may still be struggling to gain an emotional or spiritual equilibrium. The experience of the camp or conference may be exactly what they need at this critical juncture of their lives.

To be alert to their needs does not mean to make a fuss about them or to pamper them. It is always better to treat them on the assumption that they are adequate to their responsibilities as parents and participants.

Children who are hungry for a mother or a father will often, and quite understandably, attach themselves to the mothers or fathers of other families. Other parents who observe such a fixation might quietly arrange also to befriend the child. This will relieve the first "foster parent" of some of the responsibility and let the child know that he has more than one friend.

Families with Handicapped Children

In recent years a number of specialized organizations have been developed to help families whose children are handicapped by blindness, hearing deficiencies, mental deficiencies, and crippling malformations or diseases. The National Council of Churches has developed a Committee on the Education of Exceptional Persons which is helping the denominations to include such people in their programs. Further information can be secured from the Committee at the National Council headquarters—475 Riverside Drive, New York 27, N. Y.

In larger metropolitan areas, some of these agencies sponsor special family events. It is the responsibility of the church to call these to the attention of its parishioners who need them. It is also the responsibility of the church to work with such agencies, to help them meet the deepest spiritual needs of the families they serve.

In many instances, however, families whose children have handicaps will need to be included in the church-sponsored events along with the other families. This will require considerable grace (using that word in its highest spiritual meaning) and skill on the part of the staff leadership.

Step one is to include in the invitation such families as the staff feel will profit from the experience. The staff should check their own attitudes about such a venture. Have they the patience and love required by the special needs of such families? Does at least some of the staff have some experience and insight in working with the particular difficulties involved? What special problems regarding the site, facilities, and program will the presence of a family with these certain handicaps create and how can they be met?

The invitation to families with handicapped children may have to be specific and direct, on a person-to-person basis. If the parents have tended to become ingrown because of feelings of guilt and shame, it may take a bit of special effort to make them feel genuinely welcome and accepted. Where parents are oversensitive and self-conscious about the handicap, however, it should be made clear from the very beginning that, in the main, they are going to be treated as every other family and that they will be expected to fit into the activities and responsibilities.

Step two is for the staff to set the mood and spirit which will guide the other families in understanding and accepting the family with the handicapped child. The basic principle to be kept in mind here is that every one of us, even the so-called "normal" person, has certain strengths and certain weaknesses. These weaknesses may be considered our "handicaps," but we learn to live with them, and not to let them get us down.

In much the same way, members of a family with a more severe handicap must be helped by real experience and fellowship to live with their handicap. With the loving, but at the same time challenging, support of a group of Christian families, many handicapped families have been helped to a new-found freedom which has made possible amazing growth for both parents and children.

The presence of a family with a handicapped child is often one of the most powerful dynamics in the camp or conference experience. All the families will grow in understanding and compassion. Other children will often have their first encounter with persons so limited. The whole setting adds a depth to the meaning of Christian community.

Three-generation Families

In both family camps and family conferences it has been the policy to urge the entire household that normally lives together to participate. This would include grandparents, maiden aunts, bachelor uncles, or any other relatives living in the household.

Grandparents can often be helped as much as parents by the experience of living with other families under the inspiration of a Christian fellowship. They gain some insight into the dynamics of family interaction and may gain some objectivity as they live with other families.

There is a further advantage to having some grandparents present. In our time mobility and many other factors make it impossible for some children to know their grandparents well. Many children will flock to an older person and often the grandparents in a conference will find themselves surrounded by many not their direct descendants.

Older Couples

With the increasing attention focused on persons in retirement and the older years, we have been forced to be concerned about their family relationships. We have also been forced to recognition of the fact that many of these couples have lively interests and greater capabilities than we have dared imagine. Conferences especially focused on the older couple have proved immensely worthwhile.

The same procedures outlined earlier can be followed in developing a conference for older couples. The schedule will need to be made for a more leisurely pace, but you can be sure to count on some lively discussion.

One of our happy recollections is of a camp for "over 65's." They had a merry fiddler in their group, and their square dance was one of the jolliest we have ever attended.

OTHER TYPES OF FAMILY EXPERIENCES

Churches are showing increasing imagination and ingenuity in using some of the natural interests of families as vehicles for strengthening and enriching the quality of Christian living within families. There are many varieties of experiences which the alert church will seize and transform to help in the nurture of Christian families. Space will permit us only the brief mention of four types of projects on which there has been scattered experimentation in recent years.

Family Tours and Caravans

With vacations on wheels becoming increasingly popular, some churches are organizing family tours or caravans. A group of families in cars, equipped with either tents or trailers, will cover a route together. They visit religious and historical shrines and places of scenic beauty along the way and plan to stop together each evening. Often they visit home mission projects, church colleges, and other churches which make the work of the church in the world today become alive. Some of the values of living and traveling together make the caravan seem like a camp on wheels. Many of the suggestions given earlier about planning the family camp are applicable to planning for the family caravan.

One Michigan church found ten of its families planning trips to the Rockies. With some advance planning, they agreed to converge on Yellowstone Park on a certain date and spend a week together. They had the shared experience of seeing the awe-inspiring wonders of the park and of camping together for the period. This kind of fellowship makes for real enthusiasm in the ongoing work of the church, as well as providing intrinsic benefit to the families involved.

Trail, Canoe and Boat Trips

Families whose children are adolescents often will like to back-pack or burro-pack into the wilderness. Others will like to use canoes or boats as their mode of transportation. When churches find some of their families engaging in such activities, it is time for the churches to ask, "How can we help our families get the most out of these experiences?"

One church developed a year-round interest group on camping. Meeting monthly throughout the winter, they compared notes on equipment, trails, places to see, and experimented with camp recipes. Their meetings included family singing, games, and worship. By the time they hit the trail in the summer they were already a well seasoned crew.

Groupings by Vocation

With the increasing concern in our churches with the ministry of the laity, especially in relation to their vocation, some churches have turned to the family conference as an ideal method for dealing with some of the problems uncovered. It is well known that certain types of work place greater stress on families. The church can bring together these families who are in the same predicament and help them. Some of the families which have been helped by such conferences are those of: armed services personnel, businessmen who travel, businessmen overseas, physicians, teachers, clergy.

Families of any workers who face unusual hours or working conditions may need the help of the church. Certain professions where the husband is thrown in frequent contact with women, or where he must engage in secret or confidential work, have their own peculiar problems. If the gospel of Christ is to become relevant in the lives of these people, it must be a saving and healing force at these very specific and difficult points.

Work Projects

Family camps and conferences have been challenged by some who feel that they make an idolatry of family fun and fellowship in a world that is sick and torn and bleeding. Such folks insist that Christian families should make manifest a more sensitive concern for their fellow man.

These persons claim that a Christian family conference becomes most effective when families cease being concerned about their internal relationships and unite in a common effort to serve some area of need.

With this in mind, the American Friends Service Committee and a few other groups have built into their family conference programs work periods during which all the families will build a playground in a depressed area, or rehabilitate a community center.

Experiences with workcamps among youth and college students would indicate that this is a promising type of experience for families. A word of caution needs to be added, however, to remind us that a *family* workcamp needs to keep its primary focus on the quality of the interaction within the family and to help the family grow in its Christian witness.

The temptation must be avoided to exploit family labor simply to develop church camp and conference grounds. The study and discussion periods that characterize all good work projects should be concerned with the impact of the experience on family values and behavior.

FIVE: RESOURCES FOR PROGRAM BUILDING

Good leaders will bring to camp their own rich backgrounds and personalities and will use a variety of resources in their own unique ways. The following resources are suggested as supplements because of their proven value.

ADMINISTRATION AND PRACTICE

American Baptist. Hanson, Joseph J., *Family Camp Program and Resource Guide* (75¢). American Baptist Department of Family Life, Valley Forge, Pa.

American Camping Association. *Family Camp Standards* (10¢). Bradford Woods, Martinsville, Ind.

Y.M.C.A. Beckhard, Richard, *How to Plan and Conduct Workshops and Conferences* ($1.00). Association Press.

NATURE STUDY AND ACTIVITIES

The Basic Science Education Series, more than 60 titles (48¢ or 52¢ each). Rowe, Peterson and Co., Evanston, Illinois.

Field Guide Series ($4.50 each). Houghton Mifflin.

- *A Field Guide to Animal Tracks,* Olaus Murie
- *A Field Guide to Birds of Britain and Europe,* Roger Tory Peterson, et. al.
- *A Field Guide to the Ferns,* Boughton Cobb
- *A Field Guide to Rocks and Minerals,* Frederick H. Pough
- *A Field Guide to the Mammals,* W. H. Burt and R. P. Grossenheider

Foster, Virgil, *Close-up of a Honey Bee* ($3.00). William R. Scott, 1960.

Golden Nature Guides (paper, $1.00; hardcover, $2.50). Golden Press.

Birds — *Reptiles and Amphibians*
Fishes — *Rocks and Minerals*
Flowers — *Seashores*
Insects — *Stars*
Mammals — *Trees*
Nature Crafts — *Weather*

Lowdermilk, W. C. *Conquest of the Land Through 7,000 Years* (Bulletin No. 99, free). U.S. Department of Agriculture, Washington 25, D. C.

McKready, Kelvin. *A Beginner's Guide to the Stars.* G. P. Putnam's Sons, 1924.

Storer, John H. *The Web of Life* (50¢). New American Library of World Literature, 501 Madison Ave., New York 22, N. Y.

Zim Books (paper, $1.00; cloth, $3.50). Simon and Schuster.

Flowers, Herbert S. Zim and Alexander C. Martin
Insects, Herbert S. Zim and Clarence A. Cottam
Trees, Herbert S. Zim and Alexander C. Martin

CRAFTS

Barbour, Russell and Ruth. *Religious Ideas for Arts and Crafts* ($2.75). Christian Education Press, 1959.

Carhart, Arthur H. *The Outdoorsman's Cookbook* ($2.95). Macmillan, 1955.

Cooking Out-of-Doors ($1.95). National Equipment Service, 830 Third Ave., New York 22, N. Y.

Hammett, Catherine T. *Your Own Book of Campcraft* (35¢). Affiliated Publishers, Pocket Books, 630 Fifth Ave., New York 20, N. Y.

Ickis, Marguerite and Esh, Reba Selden. *The Book of Arts and Crafts* ($4.95). Association Press, 1954.

Kephart, Horace. *The Camp Cookery* ($2.49). Macmillan.

Patterson, Doris T. *Your Family Goes Camping* (paper, $1.50; cloth, $2.50). Abingdon, 1959.

Southard, Helen F. *Family Activities with Other Families* (75¢). National Board, Y.W.C.A., 600 Lexington Avenue, New York 22, N. Y.

Stinson, Thelma. *Native 'n Creative* (40¢). Methodist Board of Education, Camping Service, P.O. Box 871, Nashville 2, Tenn.

Sunset Ideas for Family Camping ($1.75). Lane Book Co., Menlo Park, Calif.

Sunset Ideas for Outdoor Family Fun in the West ($1.95). Lane Book Co., Menlo Park, Calif.

Wilson, George T. *Family Camping* ($1.00). Laacke and Joys Co., 1433 N. Water St., Milwaukee 2, Wis.

RECREATION

Eisenberg, Helen and Larry. *The Family Fun Book* ($2.95). Association Press, 1953.

Fun and Festival Series (75¢ each). Friendship Press.

Fun and Festival from China, Margaret G. Hummel

Fun and Festival from India, Pakistan, and Ceylon, Irene Wells and Jean Bothwell

Fun and Festival from Latin America, Ella Huff Kepple

Fun and Festival from the U.S. and Canada, Larry Eisenberg

Harbin, Elvin O. *Fun Encyclopedia* ($4.95). Abingdon.

Harbin, Elvin O. *Games for Boys and Girls* (paper, $1.35; cloth, $2.00). Abingdon, 1951.

Millen, Nina. *Children's Games from Many Lands* (paper, $1.95; cloth, $2.95). Friendship Press.

Schlingman, Edward L. *The Recreation Job in Camp and Conference* (75¢). Christian Education Press.

MUSIC

Most denominations have prepared their own camp and conference songbook. Consult your headquarters, or write to the Cooperative Recreation Service, Inc., Delaware, Ohio.

Thomas, Edith Lovell. *The Whole World Singing* (paper, $1.95; cloth, $2.95). Friendship Press.

CHRISTIAN NURTURE IN FAMILIES

Auerbach, Aline B. *The Why and How of Discipline* (40¢). Child Study Association of America, 1957.

Bro, Margueritte Harmon. *When Children Ask* ($3.50). Harper, 1956.

Brown, Leslie W. and Winifred. *The Christian Family* ($1.00). Association Press, 1959.

Channels, Vera. *The Layman Builds a Christian Home* ($1.95). Bethany, 1959.

Duvall, Evelyn Millis. *Facts of Life and Love for Teen-agers* (35¢). Popular Library, 355 Lexington Ave., New York 7, N. Y.

Eckert, G. Ralph. *Sex Attitudes in the Home* (35¢). Popular Library, 1958.

Levy, John and Munroe, Ruth. *The Happy Family* ($3.00). Knopf, 1954.

Little, Sara. *Learning Together in the Christian Fellowship* ($1.25). John Knox, 1956.

Mace, David Robert. *Success in Marriage* ($2.95). Abingdon, 1958.

Mace, David Robert. *Whom God Hath Joined* ($2.00). Westminster, 1953.

Maynard, Donald M. *Your Home Can Be Christian* (paper, $1.00; cloth, $2.00). Abingdon, 1952.

Spoerl, Dorothy. *Tensions Our Children Live With* ($3.50). Beacon, 1959.

Stewart, Maxwell S. (ed.). *The Growing Family:* A Guide for Parents ($3.50). Harper, 1955.

Thompson, William T. *An Adventure in Love* ($1.25). John Knox, 1956.

Thompson, William T. *Adventures in Parenthood* ($1.45). John Knox, 1959.

Werner, Hazen G. *Christian Family Living* ($1.00). Abingdon, 1959.

Wolf, Anna W. M. *Helping Your Child to Understand Death* (60¢). Child Study Association, 1958.

Wyckoff, D. Campbell. *In One Spirit:* Senior Highs and Missions (paper, $1.95; cloth, $2.95). Friendship Press.

Wynn, J. C. *How Christian Parents Face Family Problems* ($2.50). Westminster, 1955.

WORSHIP AND BIBLE STUDY

Anderson, Bernhard W. *Unfolding Drama of the Bible* (50¢). Association Press, 1957.

Bowman, Clarice M. *Worship Ways for Camp* ($3.50). Association Press, 1955.

Gebhard, Anna Laura and Edward. *Guideposts to Creative Family Worship* ($2.50). Abingdon, 1953.

Lentz, Richard E. *Christian Worship by Families* (75¢). Bethany, 1957.

Pease, Dorothy Wells. *Altars Under the Sky* ($1.50). Abingdon, 1957.

Pease, Dorothy Wells. *Meditations Under the Sky* ($1.50). Abingdon, 1957.

FAMILIES WITH SPECIAL NEEDS

Carlson, Bernice and Ginglend, David R. *Play Activities for the Retarded Child* ($4.00). Abingdon, 1961.

"The Church's Ministry and Persons with Special Needs." *International Journal of Religious Education*, special issue, February, 1962 (75¢).

Foster, Virgil E. (ed.). *The Church and the Handicapped* (40¢). National Council of Churches, 1954.

How to Help the Hard of Hearing Child in Your Schoolroom (25¢). New York League for the Hard of Hearing, 480 Lexington Ave., New York 17, N. Y.

Palmer, Charles E. *The Church and the Exceptional Person* ($1.75). Abingdon, 1961.

Spock, Benjamin. *On Being a Parent of a Handicapped Child* (25¢). National Society for Crippled Children and Adults, 2023 W. Ogden Ave., Chicago 12, Ill.

AUDIO-VISUAL RESOURCES

The Audio-Visual Resource Guide ($2.95), published by the National Council of Churches, lists and evaluates over two hundred films and filmstrips under the heading "The Christian Family."

For family conferences, it is usually wise to have a few extra films on the wonder of nature or family life, in case inclement weather forces the children to stay indoors.

APPENDICES

A. SITE CHECK LIST

B. A TYPICAL DIRECTOR'S LETTER

C. A FAMILY PORTRAIT

D. A LETTER FOR PARENTS OF YOUNGER CHILDREN

E. FRAME FOR FOLDING BABY CRIB

F. A FAMILY CAMP COVENANT

A. SITE CHECK LIST

This is for use of the sponsoring committee in selecting an adequate site in conformity with the standards of the Committee on Camps and Conferences of the National Council of Churches and the American Camping Association. *Committees interested in purchasing and developing a site of their own should get in touch with the site development consultant of their own denomination or of the National Council of Churches' Committee on Camps and Conferences.*

Location

	YES	NO
1. Is the site removed from populated areas and distracting resorts?	☐	☐
2. Is the site free from dangerous hazards and adequately drained?	☐	☐
3. Are there sufficient space and adequate natural resources for the type of program intended? (For a camping program, allow one acre per camper.)	☐	☐

Facilities

	YES	NO
1. Are tents, cabins, or shelters in safe condition and constructed in accordance with the building codes of the locality?	☐	☐
2. Are there adequate buildings or shelter for program activities, even in inclement weather?	☐	☐
3. Are buildings heated for cool or damp weather?	☐	☐
4. Do sleeping accommodations allow complete privacy for each family unit?	☐	☐
5. Are doorways, doorhandles, drinking fountains, etc., accessible and safe for children?	☐	☐
6. Is there a safe play area for smaller children?	☐	☐
7. Are waterfront areas or swimming pools located, constructed, and equipped in compliance with applicable laws; or do they meet the standards of a recognized water safety agency such as the Y.M.C.A., the American Camping Association or the American Red Cross?	☐	☐

Food Service

YES NO

1. Are water and milk supplies certified safe? ☐ ☐
2. Are there adequate refrigeration and other facilities for proper storage of food? ☐ ☐
3. Is the food preparation area adequate in size, clean, and protected from insects and rodents? ☐ ☐
4. Do dishwashing procedures and care of food equipment comply with local sanitary laws or meet approved practices? ☐ ☐
5. Is garbage and waste disposal handled in a manner approved by health officials? ☐ ☐

Health, Sanitation, and Safety

1. Do plumbing and sanitary facilities meet all applicable legal requirements? ☐ ☐
2. Is there an adequate supply of hot water? ☐ ☐
3. Is there a shower head for each fifteen campers or other facilities for bathing with warm water? ☐ ☐
4. Are there toilet facilities for both sexes? ☐ ☐
5. Is there a toilet seat for each ten campers? ☐ ☐
6. Are toilets clean and flyproof? ☐ ☐
7. Are there handwashing facilities near toilets? ☐ ☐
8. Is there a health center with facilities for isolating ill persons? ☐ ☐
9. Is there a nurse or doctor in attendance? (A doctor should always be available on call if a nurse is on the site.) ☐ ☐
10. Is emergency transportation always available? ☐ ☐

B. A TYPICAL DIRECTOR'S LETTER

(An earlier letter had been sent acknowledging the receipt of the registration fee, enclosing a "portrait sheet," and telling something about the director's family.)

Dear Folks:

It won't be long now! That is, not long till we all get together at Family Camp.

It will please all who have been at camp with them before to know that Sam and Tillie will be our Camp Naturalist and Nurse.

Just in case you haven't spent many nights in a well-ventilated cabin recently, don't forget Bill's suggestion to bring at least two blankets for each person. Each cabin has one convenience outlet in addition to the center light, in case your bedding is electrified.

Other things that sometimes come in handy are a few clothespins, raincoats, sand toys, a clip-board for sketching, scissors and old crayons for the "small fry," musical instruments, and hobby tools—including elementary woodworking tools (if you're not too particular about them), such as saw, hammer, plane, small square, and a rule or tape.

One of the things we like to do at Family Camp is for each family to make a sign to identify their cabin. It all helps to get acquainted and also gives a chance for a little originality if you want to make a play on your name, home town, etc. You may want to dream up an idea for yours while en route, or even make it at home. If so, we'd suggest using a piece of light cardboard not over 12" x 16".

Old campers know we always have a "Family Fun Night" toward the end of camp. The most successful "acts" have been short skits put on by an entire family—or all members old enough to participate. A little advance notice may give you time to come up with one that will "bring down the house."

In case you want to leave your address with a friend, it's (post office address). *The telephone is* (phone number).

We'll be seeing you Sunday afternoon, August 22, between 2 and 4—in time to "set up housekeeping" in your cabin before dinner at 5:45—starting a week your family will long remember.

Sincerely,

P.S. Borrowing an idea from last year, we'd like to suggest that while en route to camp you make up words to fill in the blanks below. At dinner Sunday evening each family will get to sing their version. (Anyone who can't sing well can have more fun by singing LOUD!) Here 'tis—here's a sample to give you the idea—

Hi Ho! Hi Ho!	*Hi Ho! Hi Ho!*
It's off to camp we go;	*It's off to camp we go;*
_____ _____ _______ ____	*We'll load our trunk*
_______ ___ ________ ____	*With all our junk;*
Hi Ho, Hi Ho!	*Hi Ho, Hi Ho!*

C. A FAMILY PORTRAIT SHEET

Families enrolling for a Family Life Camp are asked to furnish information to assist the directors in their planning. The camp staff will provide the major leadership, but campers are asked to help also, as their talents, interests, and experience may be needed. In filling out the following portrait, don't be so modest that you conceal your abilities.

__________ __________ __________ __________ __________

(Family Name) (Father's 1st Name) (Nickname) (Occupation) (Other Training)

__________ __________ __________ __________

(Home address—street) (City) (Home Phone) (Name of Home Church)

__________ __________ __________ __________

(Mother's 1st Name) (Nickname) (Training & Experience) (Present Occupation)

____

(Children's names, nicknames, ages, grades just completed)

____________________ This will be our _____ year in Family Camp.

We would like to know your talents and interests. Would you please write in the name of the family member interested in the listed activities? Put an "X" before activities you want to do as a family. Don't be modest!

Activity	Interested In Learning	Some experience	Have been Leader	Activity	Interested In Learning	Some experience	Have been Leader
Square or Folk Dance				Clay Modeling			
Choir				Leather-work			
Group Singing				Plaster Molding			
Geology				Woodworking			
Star Gazing				Aluminum Etching			
Dramatics				Textile or Wood Painting			

Sketching & Painting	Nature Collections

(Other activities offered include: Swimming, horseshoes, tennis, badminton, shuffleboard, volleyball, softball, and nature hikes.)

Write in any other hobby you would like in the program: ____________

Name

Have any of you had life saving or life guard experience? ____________
Have any of you had first aid training? ____________
Have any of you had medical or nursing experience? ____________
Have any of you had leadership in Scouting? ____________
Have any of you taught Sunday school (What grades)? ____________
Have any of you played piano or organ for community singing or worship services? ____________

In the Parents' Hour with the Family Counselor, what would you like to discuss?

_______What are the facts and fallacies about normal child development?
_______How do children affect the husband-wife relationship?
_______What can we do about children's quarreling and jealousy?
_______How do we reach effective decisions and regulations in the family?
_______How can the family provide for growth and satisfactions for **all** members?
_______How can we meet the pressures put on us by neighbors and the community?
_______How can we develop proper attitudes toward work?

Suggestion of other topic: ____________

In the Parents' Hour with the Camp Minister, what would you like to discuss?

_______How much teaching of religion should we do in the home?
_______How can we teach the Bible most helpfully in our family?
_______How can the history of the church help us understand our times?
_______What Christian beliefs are essential in family living?
_______When is a family "Christian"?
_______Christian acts in daily life.

Other suggestions: ____________

How can the following help our Christian growth?

Music____________ Poetry____________ Community Responsibilities ____________ Church Activities____________

Young people (seventh grade and older) are asked to number the following subjects in the order of their preference. These may be used in a morning discussion period.

________How we got our Bible
________What Christians are to believe
________Christian service through various occupations
________Christian religious vocations open to youth
________Christian worship and prayer
________How to take a stand on moral questions

Suggestion of some other topic: ____

When this Family Portrait has been fully filled in, please return it to the director of the Family Life Camp you expect to attend.

D. A LETTER FOR PARENTS OF YOUNGER CHILDREN

Dear Parents of "Small Fry":

We have discovered that most of the 4-year-olds are at home at once in the Nursery Playyard. However, those younger and even some of the older ones need a few days to get used to playing in a fenced yard away from their family. Since we have only one week, we are asking you to prepare your children at home now for this experience so that all may enjoy the whole week.

As you make your plans for Family Conference, tell a story to your little ones each day, something like this:

> There was once a little girl named Jane who went to Family Conference with sister, mother, and daddy. They all slept together in the same house. They ate in a big dining room with lots of other daddies, mommies, boys, and girls. Every morning after breakfast when the big bell rang, all the boys and girls as big as Jane went to their own playyard to have a wonderful time digging in the sandbox and swinging on the swings that were just the right size.
>
> Mother opened the gate for Jane and the lady who played with the children said, "Good morning, Jane. Here are some children to play with you."
>
> Mother said, "Have a good time, Jane. I'm going to the place where all the mothers and daddies meet. I'll be back to get you when it's time to play in the water."
>
> Jane said, "I'll play for a while, then you come back to get me."
>
> "All right," said Mother, smiling as she closed the gate to Jane's playyard so the little children wouldn't wander away.
>
> Jane went to play in the boat that was filled with sand. Pretty soon the lady who helped the children find things to do said, "Come over to the table, children. We have a little treat for you. Here, Jane, is a glass of juice and a cookie."
>
> Jane liked the treat. Then she tried out the swing that looked like a chair. She was so happy playing that when Mother came back to get her she said, "I'd like to play some more."

Mother laughed and said, "Oh, we'll go play in the water now, then later you can come back to your playyard. How will that be?"

"Oh, yes," said Jane. "Good-by, lady. I'll be back again."

You will no doubt be able to tell better stories than this to your child. This is just a sample of the type of story which will help your child feel secure and at home in the strange surroundings. Perhaps he has a toy he would like to bring. This sometimes helps to make him feel at ease. However, it should be something for *all* the children to play with. If it is a favorite toy that he doesn't want to part with, it might prove more upsetting than helpful.

Parents are asked not to come back to the Nursery Yard until both morning seminars are over. If you are needed, rest assured that someone will come for you. Both you and your child will appreciate the extra enjoyment this pre-conference planning will give.

Sincerely,
Family Camp Directors

E. FRAME FOR FOLDING BABY CRIB

View of crib, showing how ends fold for storage

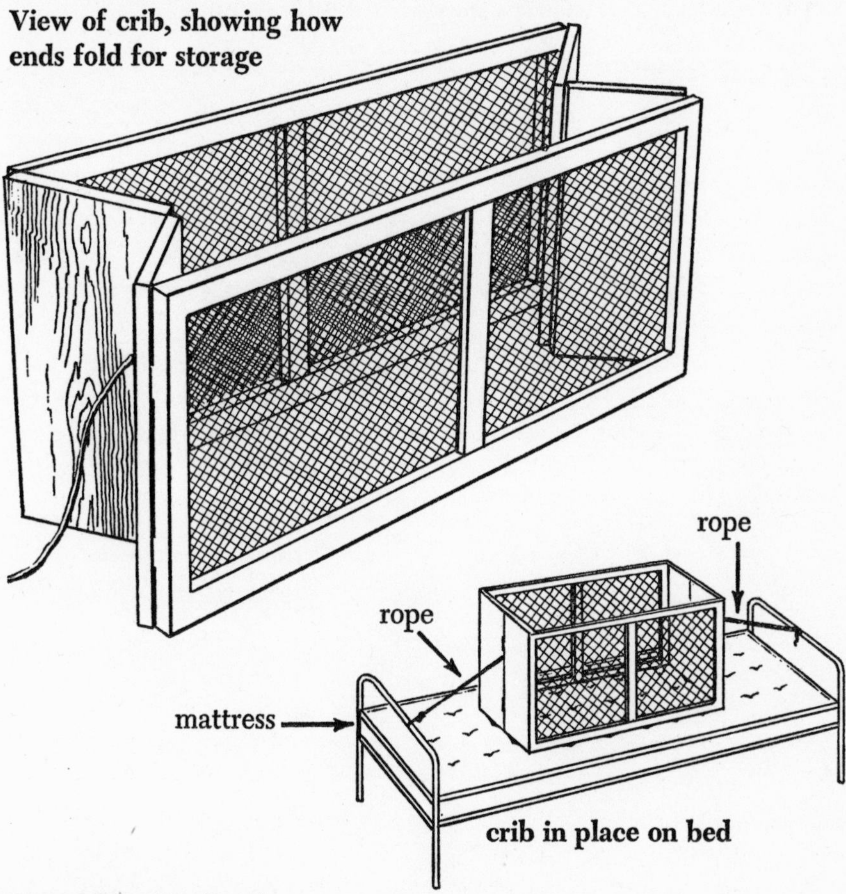

Two sides: 2′ x 4′ each
frame of 1″ x 3″ wood with center brace
screening on outside with edges covered by molding

Ends: Each end made of two pieces 12″ x 24″ x 1″

Each end hinged to fold inward for storage

Hole for heavy clothesline drilled near top hinge

Rope knotted on inside—long enough to be tied to end of cot holding frame rigidly in place on bed

This frame was developed by William T. Matters, Pilgrim Haven Camp, South Haven, Michigan.

F. A FAMILY CAMP COVENANT

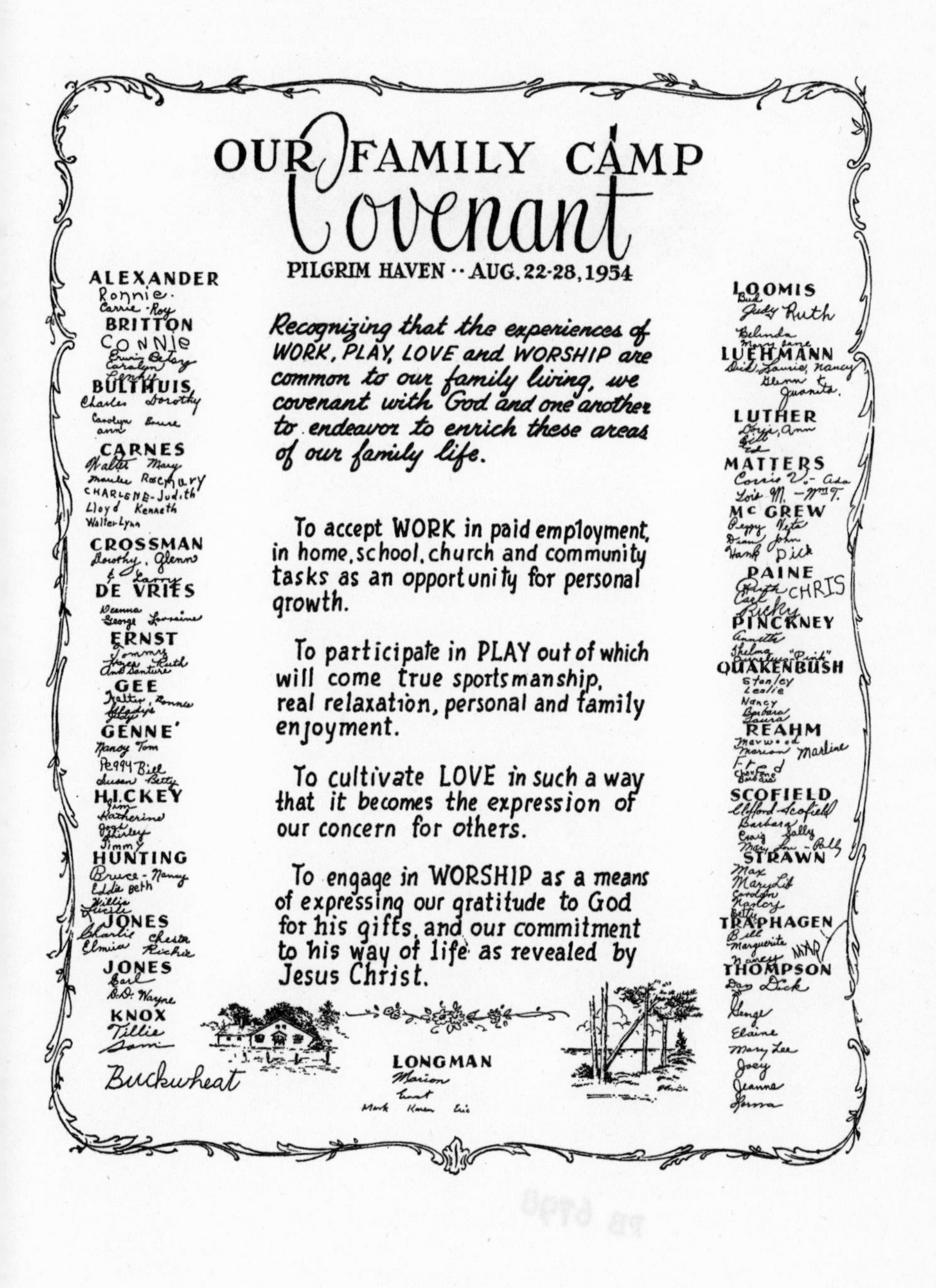

OUR FAMILY CAMP

Covenant

PILGRIM HAVEN ·· AUG. 22-28, 1954

Recognizing that the experiences of WORK, PLAY, LOVE and WORSHIP are common to our family living, we covenant with God and one another to endeavor to enrich these areas of our family life.

To accept WORK in paid employment, in home, school, church and community tasks as an opportunity for personal growth.

To participate in PLAY out of which will come true sportsmanship, real relaxation, personal and family enjoyment.

To cultivate LOVE in such a way that it becomes the expression of our concern for others.

To engage in WORSHIP as a means of expressing our gratitude to God for his gifts, and our commitment to his way of life as revealed by Jesus Christ.

ALEXANDER

BRITTON

BULTHUIS

CARNES

CROSSMAN

DE VRIES

ERNST

GEE

GENNE'

HICKEY

HUNTING

JONES

JONES

KNOX

LONGMAN

LOOMIS

LUEHMANN

LUTHER

MATTERS

McGREW

PAINE

PINCKNEY

QUAKENBUSH

REAHM

SCOFIELD

STRAWN

TRAPHAGEN

THOMPSON